LES PUGH'S
MEMORIES

T0347003

LES PUGH'S MEMORIES

COLLECTED FROM THE

STROUD NEWS & JOURNAL

First published 2008

The History Press Ltd
The Mill, Brimscombe Port
Stroud, Gloucestershire, GL5 2QG
www.thehistorypress.co.uk

© Les Pugh, 2008

The right of Les Pugh to be identified as the Author
of this work has been asserted in accordance with the
Copyrights, Designs and Patents Act 1988.

All rights reserved. No part of this book may be reprinted
or reproduced or utilised in any form or by any electronic,
mechanical or other means, now known or hereafter invented,
including photocopying and recording, or in any information
storage or retrieval system, without the permission in writing
from the Publishers.
British Library Cataloguing in Publication Data.
A catalogue record for this book is available from the British Library.

ISBN 978 0 7524 4791 9

Typesetting and origination by The History Press Ltd.
Printed in Great Britain

CONTENTS

DEDICATION

In memory of my dear wife Peggy 1916–2004

Acknowledgements

I would like to thank the following people for their help in putting this book together: Sue Smith, editor of the *Stroud News & Journal*, Andrew Barton, David Evans, Peter Higginbotham, Peckham's of Stroud, Mrs Barnfield, Dr Ray Wilson of the Gloucestershire Society for Industrial Archaeology, Gloucester Record Office, Esther Carnell and Dora Lambert of Bridgend Hostel.

FOREWORD

When Les first started sending his columns in to the *Stroud News & Journal* he was just a spring chicken in his eighties although from the sharpness of the writing and his cheery nature on the telephone we assumed he must have been at least ten years younger. When he popped into the office soon afterwards while on a visit to Stroud we amended that figure to twenty.

Over the years Les has astounded us with his ability to recollect even the tiniest details of his life and his knowledge of local history. His general knowledge of what is going on in the world often puts those of us in the news business to shame.

Les and I have lunch together once a year, a highlight in my calendar that I wouldn't miss for the world. He is always punctual – ready and waiting at the door when I arrive to collect him and always dapper in his immaculately pressed clothes, shiny shoes and Old Marlingtonian tie. There's often a bag of freshly picked vegetables or flowers waiting for me which he has just plucked from his prolific, neatly tended garden. Before long the conversation inevitably turns to his beloved Listers in Dursley where he spent many happy years in employment. And here again, without reference to any notes or prompts, Les will regale with facts and anecdotes from those days. A more charming and interesting luncheon companion it would be hard to find. We usually end with a trip to the *Stroud News & Journal* offices in Lansdown where Les likes to meet the new staff and find out all about them; if they also happen to have attended Marling School then all the better.

Unlike some people in advancing years Les doesn't view the past through rose-tinted spectacles. He has lived through hardship and as a result has learned the importance of family and friendship, both of which he holds in the highest esteem. We were all sad when Les lost his wife and childhood sweetheart, Peggy, a few years back. He had nursed her lovingly through ill health and, despite some very difficult years, only ever spoke of his situation with kindness and affection.

This collection of Les's memories is a gem and it seems unimaginable now that it might not have happened, had it not been for a sharp-eyed book editor and former *Stroud News & Journal* employee who recognised the wealth of information Les has to offer from his long and interesting life. I am delighted that the stories that have given us and our readers so much pleasure will now continue in this book for future generations.

Finally it seems we have Les's former teacher, Elsie Watts, at Eastington Primary School, to thank for his love of writing. It was she who instilled a love of composition in the young infant Pugh. I will be forever in her debt for sending such a true gentleman in our direction.

Sue Smith, Editor
Stroud News & Journal
2008

Les's parents, William and Florence, and his elder brother Percy.

1

MEMORIES OF SCHOOL AND FAMILY LIFE

MEMORIES OF THE VILLAGE SCHOOL

I should firstly explain that I am a very old Marlingtonian who has a good memory and really enjoys the physical exercise of longhand writing, as well as the mental stimulation of sharing my memories of long ago with those who choose to read them.

For our trip down memory lane we will move about a quarter of a mile from the once delightful Westfield Bridge area of the Stroudwater Canal to Churchend and Eastington C of E School.

I have vivid memories of my school days there from 1920 to 1927 and the dedicated headmaster, Mr Rowbotham ('Johnnie' to us kids), and the equally dedicated lady teachers, Elsie Watts who was the infants' teacher. She was a kind and compassionate teacher and was only about 5ft tall. She travelled to the school daily from Stroud on the 'red bus' which was driven by Dick Rene, a member of the Australian Army during the First World War, who chose to stay in this country. Miss Vaisey followed by Miss Woolford taught Standards 1 and 2 (six to seven years), Miss Benfield taught Standards 3 and 4 (eight to nine years). Standards 5, 6 and 7 were taken by the headmaster.

There were about twenty infants when I joined the school in 1920. We had slates in wooden frames and slate pencils with which we wrote our first letters and figures. We were taught the alphabet and the numbers one to ten. We also made models with plasticine and had Bible stories read to us. This would be an opportune time to mention that scripture was an all-important subject throughout the whole school. Before the class teacher had marked the register, a blue tick for present and a red cross for absent, we said 'Yes Miss' or 'Yes Sir' when our name was called. After that we said *The Lord's Prayer* and sang a hymn to piano accompaniment, *There is a Green Hill Far Away* was everybody's favourite.

We were taught the Ten Commandments at a very early age and had to recite them at most scripture lessons. We were also taught that heaven and hell were actual places and

Les aged eleven, taken at his brother's wedding in Berkeley Church, 1926.

Les's mother outside Rose Cottage, West End, Eastington, 1920s.

Les's father, August 1935.

that if we kept the Ten Commandments we would go to heaven and that if we broke them we would go to hell. Sadly, by today's Christian and moral standards everybody would go to hell. A sobering thought.

To return to the teaching practice, Standards 1 and 2 occupied the small room at the back of the school where Miss Vaisey continued to teach the three R's plus the inevitable scripture.

From there we progressed to Standards 3 and 4. This was in the large room with the windows facing the east end of the church, which was divided from the other large room under the bell tower by folding glass partitions. Miss Benfield was the class teacher and segregation for pupils according to perceived ability was practical.

There were three groups, 'duffers' (colloquial Gloucestershire), 'average' and 'bright'. The last category was those considered to have scholarship potential. I was in that group. For some unknown reason my recollection of this period is somewhat hazy. Standards 5, 6 and 7 were taught in the east–west facing room under the bell tower.

Mr Rowbotham taught this group of pupils and again the chosen few had much more attention than the remainder, who would leave school at fourteen. Every village school headmaster had one overriding ambition which was to get as many of his pupils as possible to pass the scholarship exam, to gain a place at either Marling or the Girls' High School and possibly go on to university. Failing that, a place at the boys' or girls' craft schools was acceptable. In 1927, the late Ray Tudor and I gained admission to Marling School and the late Myrtle Barham to the High School.

To end this enjoyable recollection of times long past I have to say that Eastington School pupils loved general elections. The school was used as the polling station and we have a day off, hooray. On Wednesday 29 October 1924, a general election was held and a group of five or six boys, of which I was one, whose parents supported the Conservative party, sat on the churchyard wall opposite to the door under the bell tower and sang the following words to the tune of *D'ye Ken John Peel.*

> D'ye ken Sir Frank as our member new?
> We'll have Sir Frank as our member new
> At the top of the poll in the morning.

We did have Sir Frank Nelson (Conservative) at the top of the poll. Incidentally, we were very popular with the Conservative voters, especially the landed gentry who gave their coachman or chauffeur 6d or 1s to give us. We felt like millionaires.

The results of the poll were:

Sir Frank Nelson (Con) 15,973 votes
Miss Edith Picton Turberville (Lab) 7,418 votes
Mr Arthur William Stanton (Lib) 6,057 votes

My thanks to the Gloucestershire county archivist's office for the above information.

Playground Games were Fun

There is a considerable concern about obesity and lack of physical exercise in certain schools. I share this concern and have dug deep into my memory to recall the games we enjoyed when I attended Eastington C of E School in the early 1920s.

Eastington School was built in 1833 as the National School. It was a compromise satisfying both C of E and Wesleyans in the parish. Edward Wilcox was appointed headmaster in 1859 and was the first to keep a log book as ordered by the Board of Education in 1863. He had no qualified teachers but bright boys and girls became monitors at school leaving age, some after one or two years might qualify as 'pupil teachers'. These, after four years, could pass by examination into a training college or acquire the status of assistant teachers.

In 1863 day-school attendance averaged ninety-five. Absenteeism was very high with pupils taking time off to work on local farms.

The rector and his curate were voluntary helpers teaching Holy Scripture. The syllabus was limited to reading, writing, arithmetic, needlework and scripture. Edward Wilcox was known as 'the gaffer'. In 1906, John W. Rowbotham became headmaster.

There was one playground game which I recall and which I think was unique to Eastington School. It was called 'cork' and was played in the boys' playground by older boys from late spring to early autumn. It was so popular that it almost became an obsession. The boys used the large playground and the girls and infants used the smaller one.

The girls played skipping, hopscotch and tag while the infants just watched. The boys played football using a small tennis ball in the football season and a little cricket during that season. The ball used for cricket was made with odd lengths of wool wound into a very tight ball which was enclosed in a crocheted string cover. These were made by the boys' mothers. Bonds Mill was still producing cloth and scrap lengths of wool were readily available. The mill was then the main employer of Eastington people. The bat was cut and shaped from a plank of wood and was supplied by Fred Morgan whose father was a builder employing carpenters and joiners based in the Bath Road. Wooden and metal hoops were also popular, as were whip tops.

To return to the game of cork. In those far-off days most glass bottles were sealed using a cork which were in plentiful supply. The Sorbo ball had just been invented. It would bounce about four times higher than the old-fashioned rubber or tennis ball and was quite expensive and sought after. Fred Morgan supplied the one we used. To play, a tall cork, which was about 3cm in diameter and 6cm long, was placed on level, stone-free ground about 50cm from a wall. We used our caps as brushes to clear away the stones. The player stood on a line about 4m from the wall. The player threw the Sorbo ball at the cork. It had to bounce just in front of the cork, knock it over and then hit the wall and bounce back to be caught by the player.

This scored ten points and the player would continue until he knocked the cork over but did not catch the ball. This scored five points but the player was out. He was also out if he did not catch the ball at any stage of the game.

Times were so Different when I was at School

On Tuesday 24 January 2008, I was privileged to spend a morning with the teachers and pupils of Eastington C of E School at Churchend. It was an occasion which I shall always remember and cherish. For that privilege I want to thank the head teacher Malcolm Strang and his staff of dedicated lady teachers for the warm welcome given to me. I also want to thank a former head teacher, Dennis Baker, for introducing me to Mr Strang. Dennis and I are good friends and sit together when we worship at the Church of St Michael & All Angels at Eastington.

To return to a school which I left eighty years ago, to attend Marling School at Downfield, filled me with nostalgia. I spoke to the whole school in the assembly hall initially and later visited each class to mingle with, and answer questions put to me by the pupils.

The atmosphere in the whole school was one of quiet efficiency with contented and well-mannered pupils. Each one was dressed in the school uniform. I was really impressed with their smart appearance which is a credit to their parents and to the school staff.

In the seven years in which I was a pupil, from 1920 to 1927, the majority of the children were shabbily dressed, undernourished, sometimes unwashed and generally quite miserable.

Former pupils Professor Mark Cornwall, Ben Sandell and Les Pugh at the Old Marlingtonians Dinner, May 2007. (Courtesy *Stroud News & Journal*)

At that time, the residents of Eastington, with the exception of the landed gentry, farmers, small holders and skilled tradesmen, were desperately poor. There was no National Health Service and the poor were unable to call a doctor because they knew that they could not afford to pay him. Many children had gentian violet applied to their lips and faces – this was a medication to treat impetigo, which was a skin disease associated with the presence of head lice. The application was done by the 'nit nurse' on a regular basis. Sometimes the hair of both girls and boys had to be cut very short to facilitate effective treatment.

Epidemics of scarlet fever and diphtheria occurred and young children died from both of these diseases. The poorest places were Millend, Middle Street and a row of cottages at Legg's Court off Bath Road. There was no mains water supply, no sewerage disposal and no gas or electricity in these areas.

We have to be thankful that these horrific conditions no longer exist.

Les visited Eastington School in January 2008, where he was a former pupil.

Whiteshill Girls' School, 1925/26. Peggy is seated, second from right, front row.

Les and Peggy's wedding,
1 July 1939.

Les and Peggy's wedding,
1 July 1939.

Peggy with Michael and baby daughter Rosemary outside their home in Bridgend, Stonehouse, in 1951. (Courtesy *Stroud News & Journal*)

Les and Peggy. (Courtesy *Stroud News & Journal*)

Les and Peggy's daughter Rosemary, with three of Twink's puppies.

LOVE AT FIRST SIGHT FOR LES AND PEGGY

Peggy was born at Rose Cottage, The Throat, Ruscombe, on 9 June 1916. She attended Whiteshill Girls' School and was a champion athlete. After leaving Whiteshill School she attended Miss Lewis's Commercial School in Rowcroft, Stroud, and Brimscombe Polytechnic and passed her exams to become a qualified shorthand typist.

Peggy and I met on the corner of King Street and George Street, Stroud, in the summer of 1933. It was love at first sight and we became engaged on her birthday, 9 June 1936.

During the war, Peggy's mother let her new fully furnished detached house at Field Road, Whiteshill, to Mr Roland Hill, an Air Ministry executive, and came to live with us at Bridgend, Stonehouse. She was a registered foster mother and had taken several children for temporary fostering. At that time, Miss Joan Escort was responsible for placing children in foster homes and, on 18 December 1941, she brought a ten-day-old unwanted baby boy to her for fostering. Peggy and I had no children at that stage and unofficially took over Michael and brought him up as our own child. Our daughter Rosemary was born in 1951.

Peggy worked as a secretary until she retired at seventy-one. In 2001 she was admitted to Jubilee Ward of Stroud Hospital where she received caring and compassionate treatment.

When she improved she was transferred to Highborder Lodge Residential Care Home at Leonard Stanley where she received an excellent standard of care. She was readmitted to Jubilee Ward at Stroud Hospital and then The Elms Nursing Home at Elm Road, Stonehouse. She immediately felt at home there and received love, nursing care and attention of a very high standard from dedicated staff.

We, her family, would like to thank those three establishments and everyone, including visitors, who were so kind to Peggy and so helpful and considerate to us.

The Days of Hand Washing

In the period mentioned country cottages had no main service of any description. Water was obtained from a deep well sunk under the cottage before it was built. The ground floors were flagstones laid directly on the earth. A hand pump in a wooden box about 4ft high was used to raise the water. Underneath the lead spout of the pump was a stone sink with a drain hole in the bottom from which the water drained into a nearby ditch through baked-clay land drain-pipes made in a local brick yard.

Washing day in those times long past took up to four hours. Most clothes with bed sheets and pillow cases were made of white cotton and housewives took pride in the whiteness of their washing. This was achieved by boiling the washing in a furnace sometimes referred to 'a copper' although it was made of cast iron. It held about 2-3 gallons of water to which two handfuls of washing soda had been added.

The furnace was heated by a wood or slack coal fire underneath it and was covered by a wooden lid. It took about two hours to boil after which the washing was transferred to a galvanised-steel bath. This was carried out using a stout piece of wood which was known as a copper stick to lift the garments, sheets and pillow cases into the bath of cold water, into which a blue bag containing a cube of Reckitts Blue had been immersed. The bluing was necessary to obtain the brilliant whiteness desired by the housewives who took a pride in their washing.

Moving on to the bubble and squeak which was always eaten on washing days because there was insufficient time to cook a full meal. Double portions of vegetables, generally potatoes and cabbage, were cooked on Sundays and half was put aside to be mashed and fried in a cast-iron frying pan with a little dripping on the kitchen range. It was cooked slowly until it became crisp and was eaten with slices of cold meat cut from the joint which had been roasted on Sunday.

DIY Wireless Status Symbol

I want to take you back to the 1920s when owning a wireless set was the status symbol of the day. From 1920 to 1927 when I was a pupil at Eastington C of E School, Mr J. Rowbotham, the headmaster, would read extracts from the daily newspaper to us.

Wireless telegraphy was one subject I found most interesting. I was fascinated by the subject, although lack of family finances meant that all I could do was to read about it. However, there were one or two enthusiasts in the village who built their own receiver. I knew them quite well.

The principle involved certain types of mineral ore, which when placed in contact with certain metals or other minerals, acted as rectifiers or detectors of oscillations transmitted. The detector in effect separated the high- and low-frequency components of the oscillations picked up by the aerial. IT provided an easy path to earth for the high-frequency component while the low-frequency component operated the sound produced directly, in this case primitive headphones.

The design of such sets were obtained from the *Wireless Constructor* and *Wireless World* magazines. The components used were obtained from specialist shops or by post from the manufacturers such as A.C. Cossor, Dubilier, Marconi, Mullard and Burndept. The receiving aerial and the earth wire were items on which successful reception or failure depended.

There were strict regulations imposed by the Postmaster General on the total length of the aerial. It was L-shaped and the combined height and length was restricted to 100ft. The horizontal span would generally be about 75ft with a 25ft downlead.

It was usually attached to a chimney at one end and to the top of a 30ft wooden scaffold pole at the other which was let into the ground about 3ft and supported by guy wires.

The earth wire presented quite a problem to most people. This was overcome by digging a hole some 3ft deep into which was sunk a galvanised steel pipe if one was available, or failing that, a cast-iron rainwater downpipe. The connecting point for the earth wire was cleaned off with a file and the wire attached with a suitable clip. To ensure a good 'earth' at all times, it was customary to keep the area around the pipe well watered in dry weather.

Reception of the signal was controlled by the distance of the transmitter from the receiver and the direction of the aerial. Selection was impossible and in Eastington all enthusiasts I knew received the signal from Cardiff.

My family didn't own a wireless set until the early 1930s. By then crystal sets were less popular and valve-operated sets, first with external and then with internal loud speakers were being produced in quantity. The fist set we used was made by the American Philco Corporation and was known as 'the people's set'. It had four valves, the casing was made of black bakelite and it cost £5 which was a lot of money in those days.

Les Pugh's cousin, Robert H. Pugh, in the USA.
He was stationed in Gloucestershire 1943-44.

Bob and Florence on their wedding day,
20 December 1947.

PICTURE A MOVING EXPERIENCE

The year was 1919, I was four years old and living in the small cottage near Whitminster House in which I was born. The First World War had just ended and demobilised soldiers who had been lucky enough to have survived the carnage and horrors of trench warfare were returning to the villages of their birth. As a very young boy this had no significance for me because, being born during the war, I had grown up to accept the prevailing conditions as normal. However, there is one particular, although insignificant occasion which is clearly embedded in my memory; no doubt because of its connection with both my mother's and father's families.

This was an exhibition of a new invention called moving picture. It was held in a barn adjacent to the Bell Inn on Frampton Green. The barn windows were covered with hessian sacks to exclude the light and a large, white sheet on to which the pictures were to be projected was hung at the far end opposite to the door. The barn soon filled with people who paid 1d to gain admission. Most of them had seen still pictures projected from glass slides as a 'magic lantern' but could not understand how a moving picture could be produced and were as enthralled as I was.

One of the films pictured emigrants leaving Liverpool or Southampton for the USA on the steamship *Berengaria*. This was of great interest to both my mother and father. At the beginning of the last century and up to the time of the First World War, the New World across the Atlantic Ocean had everything to offer to those adventurous enough to leave the land of their birth and seek their fortune there.

My mother, Florence Broom, then of Twigworth and previously of Nether Compton near Yeovil, and my father, William George Pugh, also of Twigworth and previously of Castle Morton in Worcestershire, were children of small tenant farmers and each had five or six brothers and sisters.

In the late 1880s and early 1990s the relatively poor country people, generally small tenant farmers and smallholders, were unable to support their large families when they left school so it became customary for the boys to work for rich 'gentlemen farmers' and the girls to go into domestic service at the large mansions of the aristocracy – both provided a job and living accommodation.

These conditions, neither of which had much prospect, were responsible for members of both the Broom and Pugh families availing themselves of the 'assisted' passage to North America. They travelled 'steerage' class below the vessel's waterline on the great *Cunard* and *White Star* ocean liners then sailing regularly between Southampton, Liverpool and New York. The names of these liners which come immediately to mind are the *Aquitania, Berengaria, Caronia* and *Lusitania*. As previously mentioned the liner featured on the emigration film was the *Berengaria*. It was on this ship and others similar to it that my mother's brothers, Harry, Percy and Jack Brown, and her sister, Mabel, had sailed at different times into the great unknown to start a new life in Schenectady, Massachusetts. At the same time my father's brother, Charles H. Pugh, and his sisters, Leah and Rachel Pugh, also made the same journey with their destination being Springfield, Illinois. While I was then too young to know why my parents were upset I now understand their distress

Les Stone's Concert Party at the Gaumont Palace Cinema, Stroud, September 1935.

when they realised their closely knit families were inexorably disintegrating due to the prevailing harsh economic climate and the lack of prospects in the United Kingdom.

On 17 August 1936, I was on holiday at Southsea with my fiancée Peggy and we took a boat trip on the paddle steamer *Whippingham* to Southampton. There, on Southampton Water lay the rusting hulk of the once-great *Berengaria* now awaiting her last journey to the ship-breaker's yard. This took me back once again to my memories of the film shown in Frampton and I felt saddened that such a beautiful ship was now of no further use.

I am gladdened to say that all members of the Broom and Pugh families made a success of their adventure and became proud citizens of the USA. However, their love of old England still prevailed and they all kept in touch with the few family members still left here and made numerous visits starting in the early 1950s.

Sadly, all the families who have emigrated have now passed away. Thankfully, their parents' affinity with their mother country was absorbed by their children and grandchildren, many of whom still take holidays here and are sorry that their forebears had, through sheer necessity, to leave the beauty of Gloucestershire and the Cotswold hills to seek a new life in the USA.

Miss Iris Apperley's Dancers before they appeared on stage at the Gaumont Palace Cinema, Stroud, in 1935. Peggy Pugh (née Cratchley) is second from the left.

Miss Fry Apperley's dancers, 1935. Peggy Pugh (née Cratchley) is second from the left.

Happy Times at the Old Palace

I recently visited the Warehouse night club in Stroud so that I could see what had been done to convert the old Gaumont Palace Cinema and later the once-popular Mecca Bingo Hall. I was very impressed by the complete transformation.

As you all know I am a very old man and recall being taken by pony and trap with my parents in the early 1920s to a Christmas pantomime staged in the old Palace Theatre, which was demolished when the Gaumont Palace Cinema was built in the mid-1930s. I vividly recall entering the old theatre with my parents. To my amazement the still visible 'Front Stalls Entrance' appears above the doorway first used 100 years ago or more. The Palace Theatre, although small, was an exact reproduction of the popular theatres of that era.

In those days the George Tap Inn was located where the entrance to the shopping precinct now stands, and employed an 'ostler' who looked after the ponies of customers. Soon after the Gaumont Palace Cinema was opened by Jesse Matthews in the mid-1930s, a very public-spirited and talented amateur actor, Len Stone, arranged a charity stage show.

In Len's 1935 production, the dancers were members of Miss Iris Apperley's dancing school. My wonderful wife, who was then Peggy Cratchley, attended Iris's classes.

Extreme Winter Tales

There was a real old-fashioned Christmas in 1927. Christmas Day began with pouring rain and ended with driving snow. By nightfall on Boxing Day, drifts of several feet deep were in various places in Eastington.

In 1929 the Stroudwater Canal was frozen over with ice up to 5in thick and I learned to skate on it. The skates had a wooden body with the steel blade secured to the bottom of it. In those days everyone wore leather boots in the winter, and a wood screw attached to the heel of the skate was screwed into the heel of the boot with leather straps around the instep and ankle.

The first winter of the Second World War was the coldest since that of 1895. From Christmas Day 1939 to February 1940 there was a frost on forty-nine days or nights with the night of 21 January being the coldest. The temperature on this occasion fell to minus 17 degrees centigrade, 2 degrees Fahrenheit. Freezing rain on the night of 27 January brought a sight never to be forgotten – telephone wires became encased in cylinders of ice over 1in thick in diameter and trees were weighted down with the glazed frost that continued until the first few days of February.

The winter of 1947 was one of the longest and coldest for between 1 January and 9 March there were fifty-three air frosts and on three occasions the temperature fell to within a few degrees of zero degrees Fahrenheit. More than 1ft of snow fell in early March and this was followed by heavy rainfall – 6.97in during the month.

Almost every new house in Bridgend had frozen pipes, ours included, and water had to be carried in buckets from one or two neighbours who had kept sufficient

The Workhouse, Eastington. (Courtesy Peter Higginbotham)

heat in their house to prevent freezing. Our house and others were flooded when the thaw occurred. The local plumber worked day and night until all the pipes were repaired. I had to make a business trip for my company to Newport in South Wales and was unable to drive past Highnam because the tide and the floods made the road to Gloucester impassable. When the tide turned in the early hours of the next morning the police allowed the traffic to proceed.

The worst blizzard this century hit Gloucestershire on Saturday 29 December 1962 when drifting snow whipped up by gale-force winds throughout the night, left many villages cut off by the following morning. Further falls of snow in the next few days quickly undid the work of road clearing in the county. Many villages remained isolated for more than three days. Parts of Gloucestershire experienced up to 30 degrees of frost and a lot of homes were without electricity or gas.

The Gloucestershire Highways Committee learned at its meeting at the end of January 1963 that more than 5 million cubic yards of snow had been removed from the county's roads. Further falls of snow occurred in early February, and towards the middle of the month. The Severn Iris, a tug travelling up and down the Berkeley Canal was used as an ice-breaker to ensure that the waterway remained open for other vessels using it. One of the ships docking at Sharpness during this cold spell carried salt for the Gloucestershire roads. The winter of 1962/63 was the coldest in the twentieth century.

I drove a car to Dursley and back every working day from 1940 until 1980 and road conditions during this period were the worst I have every experienced and, like the majority of motorists, I had to purchase snow chains which were attached to the rear wheels of the Hillman Minx I was driving at that time.

To end this account of times long past I would like to acknowledge an article written by Peter D. Bailey in the *Dursley Gazette* centenary supplement published in 1978.

Recalling the Abject Poverty

In the late 1920s and early 1930s, I lived next to the Eastington Workhouse, which is now William Morris House and was built in 1783 using Frampton brick.

My recollection of the workhouse was as a forbidding, dismal place lived in by destitute people all of whom would have been incapable of survival on their own. There was strict segregation, with men being confined to one section and one dormitory and women receiving the same treatment. This rule caused great distress in cases where a husband and wife were admitted together but were immediately separated into their respective sections.

The clothing provided was brown-corduroy suits and caps with rough blue-flannel shirts and hob-nailed boots for the men. The women had coarse black-serge dresses, a white pinafore and cap with black-woollen stockings and heavy lace-up boots.

The discipline enforced by Mr Fletcher, the workhouse master, and his wife was strict and the living conditions were extremely spartan. As far as possible the institution was self-supporting, with the men working in the large garden and the women who were capable engaging in domestic duties and working in the laundry.

The mortality rate of the inmates was high, although the sick were treated in a separate wooden building known as the Fever Hospital. Medical care in the institution was limited to a local doctor's personal knowledge and the few medicines available. Pneumonia, scarlet fever, diphtheria, tuberculosis and cancer were the main causes of death. In winter there were few weeks in which the mortuary did not contain the corpse of some poor soul destined to receive a 'pauper's funeral.'

In addition to the regular inmates, provision was made to accommodate 'tramps' who were middle-aged, and elderly homeless men who spent what was left of their lives walking from one workhouse to another. To gain admission, the tramp had to produce a signed note stating that he had previously stayed in a workhouse and had completed an allotted task. To pay for his food and accommodation at Eastington Workhouse the tramp was required to break up stone used for road making and repair. Originally soft oolitic Cotswold limestone was used for this purpose but after the Stroudwater Canal became available, hard limestone, which I think came from Tytherington, was brought by barge up the canal and unloaded at the Stone Wharf, above the Pike Bridge and Lock.

The large pieces of hard stone were taken by horse and cart to the workhouse from the Stone Wharf. There was a separate brick building in which four or five stone-breaking cubicles had been incorporated. The front of each cubicle was formed by a cast-iron plate inclined at an angle of 45 degrees in which there were about thirty holes, 76mm in diameter. The tramp was required to break up the 50 kilos or so of stone and throw it through the holes. When it was seen that the task had been completed he had to move the stone to the adjacent stone heap. He would then be given his note by the workhouse master and would plod his weary way to the next workhouse.

To end my recollection, I would like to quote excerpts from the *History of Eastington* written by A.E. Keys and printed in the *Stroud News & Journal* in 1953. It reads:

> In 1834 Mr William Franklin was employed to value our workhouse for sale to the Wheatenhurst Union. In 1837 three guardians of the poor were appointed to represent the parishes which made up The Union. They were Arlingham, Brookthorpe, Eastington, Frampton, Fretherne, Frocester, Hardwicke, Harescombe, Haresfield, Longney, Moreton Valence, Saul, Standish and Whitminster.

This explains why many people used to refer to the establishment as 'the union' rather than 'the workhouse'. It sounded better.

Poor Forced to Resort to 'Quack Doctors'

In the early part of the last century most country people were very poor, had quite large families, were housed in rented cottages or terraced houses and existed on what could be described as 'starvation wages'. There was no National Health Service and to pay a doctor's bill was absolutely impossible. When there was illness they would seek advice form the local 'quack doctor'. Most villages had one and in Eastington it was Mr Critchley who lived in Westend. He was a very caring and compassionate elderly gentleman who would give advice to those who visited him for a few pence. He knew that the very poor would be unable to pay but never the less gave them the advice they desired. His remedies were simple and used materials which were cheap and easily available. I have very vivid memories of young children dying from diphtheria and scarlet fever at Eastington School. When the epidemics occurred, the patents' main concern was to prevent their children catching these diseases. Mr Critchley's advice was to purchase 'flowers of sulphur' which was a yellowish powder and to place a little on the palm of the hand and, with your mouth, blow it into the child's open mouth so that it covered the back of the throat and tonsils.

By today's standards it would be classed as very unhygienic, however it must have worked. Had it not I should not be writing this latest bit of nostalgia.

ANYTHING ON, SIR?

In the early 1930s almost every young man conformed to the prevailing fashion for short 'back-and-sides' haircut and a liberal application of Brylcreem. Dursley had two barber shops – Harry Beard next to Montgomery's in Silver Street and Mr Kingham whose premises were upstairs over Bloodworth's shop in Long Street. Harry Beard charged 4d for a haircut while Mr Kingham charged 'a tanner' or 6d. This meant that the bosses and businessmen had their hair cut by Mr Kingham while everyone else went to Harry Beard.

Every working day between noon and 1 p.m., which was Lister's dinner hour, there was a mad rush to get to Harry Beard's first. Men working in the iron foundry had a distinct advantage because it was nearer to Harry Beard's shop.

The moment the noon hooter (siren) sounded, those wanting a haircut would run to the check clocks, punch their number and make a mad dash up Water Street. We always called it Black Street as did most Dursley people. Harry Beard and his three assistants would be ready for the rush and the first three would sit down in the chairs provided. Harry's assistants were Les Whiting, 'Farmer' who had a club foot and walked with difficulty, and 'Badger' Atkins who was a lather boy and learning to be a barber.

On one memorable occasion when I was there, a young boy whose nickname was Chunky went to Harry Beard's for his first haircut. When asked the usual question, 'Anything on, sir?' Chunky replied, 'Only me 'at', much to the amusement of those waiting for a haircut.

2

WORKING LIFE

NO NEED FOR A CV IN THE 1930S

I have no idea why or when the Curriculum Vitae or CV started and why it replaced the long-established practice of a reference from someone who knew you well. In the case of a school leaver it was considered that a reference from the headmaster and another from a well-known professional person were all that was needed. Unlike today, regular attendance at a place of worship was practiced by the majority of country families. This meant that the natural choice for a second reference was always the minister of the place of worship involved, irrespective of whether it was the Church of England, Roman Catholic or any Non-Conformist Church.

At this stage I must state that when, in September 1931, I was interviewed by Mr George A. Lister, one of five brothers who were directors of R.A. Lister & Co. Ltd of Dursley, I had no written reference. However, this did not deter George and, after establishing that I was a former pupil of Marling School and reasonably articulate, he offered me a job in the company's iron foundry.

This, as I have previously stated, proved to be a job for life and one which I really enjoyed. In my case I never needed a written reference, but although I had already obtained a job, my father insisted that I should obtain two written references just in case my job at Lister's should be terminated and I would have to seek other employment. I have retained both references and I hope that readers will enjoy seeing what references of seventy years ago looked like. (See page 36).

The first from Mr H.W. Carter, the headmaster of Marling School, is dated 6 September 1932 and shows that I was a very average pupil with not much academic potential which justifies my career in becoming a professional foundryman.

The second one is from the Revd G.T.A. Ward, the Rector of Eastington and dated 9 September 1932. This was probably the last document signed by him because he died a few weeks later. Next to my parents, Revd Ward had the greater influence

MARLING SCHOOL, STROUD.

Report for the _Spring_ Term, 19_28_

Form _IIα_ Average Age of Form _12·6_ No. of Boys in Form _24_

Name _L. C. Page_ Age _12·7_ Position in Form _4_

68053 JO

SUBJECT	Position in Term	Position in Exam.	REMARKS	MASTER'S INITIALS
SCRIPTURE	4	7	Good.	H.D.7.
ENGLISH	6	7=	Good	C.P.D.
HISTORY	13	15	Very fair.	SEh.
GEOGRAPHY	7	3	Good.	H.D.7.
FRENCH	12	5	A steady worker: good exam result	Ju
CHEMISTRY				
PHYSICS				
NATURE STUDY	2	2	Very good	DBh
MATHEMATICS	5	3	Very Good.	H.D.7.
WRITING				
DRAWING	1	3.	Very Good	E.P.
HAND } WORK WOOD }	1		V. Good	A.Soss
GYMNASIUM			Good.	SEh.
LATIN	6	7	Good.	HWC.

No. of times Absent......_2_......No. of times Late......_1_......No. of " Stars "......_2_......

Conduct......_Excellent_......

A good Report.

HWCarter

Next Term begins......_Thurs Apl 26_......at 10 A.M.   ....
Head Master.

Marling School report, spring 1928.

Marling School Gymnasium Team, summer 1930. Les seated fourt from left, third row from back.

Marling School Second Eleven Football Team, 1930-31. Back row, left to right: Jasper Keen, Harry Beck, Les Pugh, John Short, Edwin (Cockney) Organ (Linesman). Front row: Jimmy Lewis, Bill Shipway, Dick Stephens, Fred Speke (captain), Doug Soulsby, 'Cherry' Gardiner, Ian Hughes.

From the Rev. G. T. A. WARD, M.A.,
Telephone—Stonehouse, 141.
Telegrams—Rector, Eastington.

EASTINGTON RECTORY,

nr. STONEHOUSE,

8/9/32.

GLOUCESTERSHIRE.

To those it may concern :

It gives me real pleasure to bear strong testimony to the character and trustworthiness of Leslie Charles Pugh, of this parish.

I have known Leslie Pugh since his childhood, and have carefully watched him throughout his school days, and also since he has been in his present employment.

He is steady, sensible, and reliable, and is one of the most promising boys in my whole parish.

I hope that he may obtain the employment he seeks ; if he does, I would be very, very disappointed if he did not give the completest satisfaction. I know that this is very strong testimony to give in these days ; but I give it because, (and only because) I know the boy so long and so well.

(Signed)   *G. J. A. Ward.*

Rector of Eastington.

Reference given for Les by Rev G. T. A. Ward, Rector of Eastington in 1932.

MARLING SCHOOL,

STROUD, GLOS.

September 6th., 1932.

L.C.Pugh was in attendance at this School from September, 1927, to July, 1931. In July, 1931, he passed the Cambridge School Certificate Examination, obtaining the mark of "credit" in English, Geography and French.

His record at the School was a good one and I always found him trustworthy and reliable.

H.W.Carter.   M. A. (Oxon.)

Headmaster.

FOUNDED 1887.

Reference from H. W. Carter, headmaster, Marling School, September 1932.

R.A.Lister works, 1938. (Courtesy *Stroud News & Journal*)

R.A. Lister, works 1938. (Courtesy Andrew Barton)

in my upbringing. Both parents, with myself, were regular church goers and, as was the case in those far-off days, based their mode of life as laid down in the Ten Commandments.

Returning to the CV I would like to quote from an article I read recently which stated that more than half of British workers would lie on their CVs to snare a dream job. This being the case I think that the old-fashioned reference, while outdated, was at least reliable whereas self-generated CVs certainly cannot be placed in that category.

Nostalgic Look at Foundries

The subject for this bit of nostalgia is one which gives me great pleasure, though it's tinged with sadness. Most people know that I worked as a professional foundryman in the iron foundries of that once-great company R.A. Lister & Co. Ltd of Dursley. A foundry is a workplace where metals are melted and poured into sand, or in some cases metal moulds; the interior shape of which forms the casting when the molten metal has solidified. It is one of the oldest industries dating back many thousands of years and it is believed that the process originated in China. Without the iron foundry the Industrial Revolution would not have been possible. Since that period and well into the twentieth century the iron foundry was of major importance with every possible article that was suitable being made in cast iron.

The skilled men in the industry were known as moulders and core makers who were also trained to melt their own metal in a core-melting furnace to a specification which was suited to the casting being made.

In the Lister Iron Foundries during my time, the mechanical properties as specified in BS 1452 Grades 4 and 17 were rigidly adhered to and nothing was cast until the molten metal had been sampled with a small quantity being poured to form a test bar. This was cast in an oil sand core in which there was a rectangular slot about ⅜in wide, the core being retained in a metal mould.

The contact of the molten metal with the metal mould produced a rapid cooling rate resulting in what was known as a 'chill'. When the test bar was fractured, the depth of chill indicated the chemical composition of the molten iron and its predicted ultimate tensile strength. The depth of chill was measured on a gauge and any metal not conforming was rejected and poured into the pig bed. It was this strict control of materials which was responsible for the worldwide reputation for superb quality which made Lister engines the very best in their class.

At this stage I must state that I was not a qualified metallurgist but nevertheless felt that I should do my humble best just for the sake of the hundreds of enthusiasts who cherish, maintain and exhibit vintage Lister engines and on the whole, I have no doubt, will agree with me that no other engine beats a Lister for quality and reliability.

It saddens me to have to state that, to the best of my knowledge, there is only one iron foundry of any magnitude left in the county of Gloucestershire. That is the highly mechanised and, dare I say it, a world leader in its class, namely Federal Mogul Camshaft Castings Ltd of Tutnalls, Lydney. I have always had a great respect for this company and my diary tells me that I visited the plant on 13 April 1966, when it was the British Piston Ring Co. Ltd, to evaluate their installation of CTI moulding machines made by British Moulding machines at Faversham in Kent I was impressed and advised my company to purchase similar machines for installation at our Dursley foundry.

The following is a list of once-great and prospering Gloucestershire iron foundries that have ceased to exist: The Dudbridge Iron Foundry, Bloodworths of Dudbridge, Lewis & Hole of Dudbridge, George Waller of Thrupp, J.H. & J. Daniels of Lightpill, Newman Henders of Woodchester, Hewins of Brimscombe, Gloucester Foundry Ltd of Gloucester, Fielding & Platt of Gloucester, Simon Barron of Gloucester, Herbert and Young of the Forest of Dean, Teague and Chew of the Forest of Dean, Newman Industries of Yate and at the end of 2001 the Lister Petter foundry at Dursley. I have no means of validation of the above information which emerges from my memory and would apologise for any errors or omissions.

Finally I would like to address any of my readers who once worked in any capacity in one of the foundries I have mentioned. I assure them that what they did was both constructive and rewarding although the conditions in which they worked would not be acceptable by today's standards. I respect and admire them.

I am one of the few people who obtained complete and absolute job satisfaction during the forty-nine years I worked as a foundryman and if I had my time again I would choose the same career.

Question of Safety

For this latest journey into the dim and distant past I want to return to life in the Lister's Iron Foundry during the 1930s.

Whilst I was working in the mid-1930s, Jim Harris had a horrific accident when molten cast iron virtually exploded when he poured it into a damp cast-iron mould. Jim was badly burned and was in excruciating pain because a droplet of molten cast iron had almost completely burned away his right eyeball.

I had been given basic first-aid training soon after I joined the company by the ex-Royal Navy sick-berth attendants Arthur Ivey and George Oxland who manned the work's medical centre known as the clinic. I had never witnessed anyone in such pain and distress and was unable to handle the situation. George Oxland rushed to the foundry from the clinic and I think gave Jim morphine after which he was rushed by works' ambulance to the old Royal Infirmary in Southgate Street, Gloucester, where he was given immediate treatment. Unbelievably Jim made a complete recovery in a very short time and returned to his job making cast-iron pistons with his mate Jack Sawyer.

From then on Jim and I had a special relationship because although I was unable to attend to his terribly burned eye, I did my best to comfort him which he appreciated. I never lost touch with him completely and used to visit him when he was a resident in Eastington Park old people's home in the mid-1960s.

Lister's foundry workers, 1939. Harry Brown extreme right, middle row; Jim Harris extreme right, front row. (Courtesy *Stroud News & Journal*)

To end this rather distressing reminiscence, which I think illustrates the total lack of legislation to ensure safety in the workplace at that time, had Jim been wearing protective glasses or goggles this terrible accident would not have occurred. I also wonder how much money Jim would have received if the accident had happened in the 'no win no fee' compensation-orientated society of today.

Shivers ran down my Spine

I have dug deeply into my memory cells to recall a period in the early 1930s when I helped a very nice elderly man named Harry Brown. Harry was one of Sir Ashton Lister's original workers and had worked in the iron foundry for many years and was nearing his retirement.

Howards Upper Mill had been the manufacturing base for the Dursley Pedersen Bicycle and after manufacturing ceased in 1914 the ground floor was used as the workers' mess room and that half of the basement was used as a wood-pattern store. When I started the updating of the pattern store I noted that the other half of the basement was securely padlocked and in a very dilapidated condition. Ivy had grown unchecked for many years and had covered the windows on the side of the building facing Long Street.

Towards the end of the updating exercise I said to Harry Brown, 'What is inside that old building and why is it securely padlocked?' Harry replied that he did not know what was inside and had been told that no one was allowed to enter it. This made me very interested and every time we passed the building I felt an increasing urge to see what was inside. I asked Harry again, 'Why can't we go inside?' He was adamant and said, 'Because we have been told not to'.

A few weeks later, it was wintertime; Harry was unwell and unable to come to work which meant that I had to find the patterns myself. He had a large bunch of keys, one of which he used to unlock the padlock on the mess-room door to gain entry to all the pattern stores. I found the wanted pattern immediately and could not resist the urge to try the other keys in the padlock of the dilapidated building. I looked at the padlock noting that it was much larger than the one on the mess-room door and selected the largest key on the bunch of about six keys. To my surprise it opened the lock and I was able to open the door and look inside.

What I saw was very eerie and just like a scene from a horror film. I felt my heart rate increase and cold shivers run down my spine. I summoned up enough courage to go inside only to feel what I can describe as a 'presence', something I had never felt before and it was very frightening. I do not believe in ghosts or the paranormal but have to admit that I felt an identical sensation of a 'presence' and fright when I entered Woodchester Park Mansion when, on a night exercise with the Home Guard during the dark days of the Second World War, we were told that the German invasion of Britain was imminent. I have never felt anything like this since that date but, over sixty years later, I have very vivid memories of both occasions.

To return to what I saw when I entered the room, which was in total darkness except from the light coming in from the open door. Dust-laden cobwebs were hanging from the ceiling, there were workmen's tools and half-finished Pedersen bicycle frames on the work benches, brazing torches were all over the floor and half-built wire-spoked wheels hanging on hooks from the ceiling beams. There were also workmen's enamelled tea cans on one end of the workbench and a large cardboard box half-full of spokes and a pile of rusty wheel trims.

I was only in there a few minutes but was getting ever more frightened, so I hastily walked out and locked the door. It was an experience that I wanted to forget and have never talked or written about it until now.

MORE MEMORIES OF LIFE IN THE FOUNDRY SIXTY YEARS AGO

I am recording some more memories of more than sixty years ago. The first point is that the work carried out by a foundry man is one of the very few occupations which could be described as being truly creative. Whereas engineers process an article which has already been made, foundrymen actually create an article by pouring molten metal into a void, or to use the correct technical term, the mould cavity. To explain further, a mould is an inverse reproduction of a pattern around which suitably conditioned sand has been compacted in a moulding box. In its simplest form a moulding box is in two halves with two holes drilled diagonally in lugs on the top half box which locate on to pins fixed in the bottom half box. The mould cavity produces the outside shape of the casting. Any internal shape is produced by sand cores which locate in prints attached to each half pattern.

Plate moulders were the main producers of small castings used in the manufacture of Lister engines and cream separators. A runner system by which the molten metal entered the mould cavity was attached to the pattern plate. An interesting point is that the plate moulders always worked on a piecework basis. The price paid for each casting was negotiated between the plate moulder concerned and the foundry manager, Mr Charlie Smith. Each morning the castings would be placed on the side of the metal-plated gangway where they would be inspected by a viewer and qualified staff member. Any faulty castings were rejected and the plate moulder would not be paid for them. The staff member would record the number of good castings and also the number of rejected castings and the defect which caused the rejection. This strict control ensured that the high-quality standard was always maintained.

The copy of an advertisement for Lister products also shown features the 5hp diesel engine which was introduced in 1929 and a typical hand-operated cream separator or centrifuge which the company introduced in the mid-1880s.

The dedicated foundrymen, who had worked continuously in the old foundry from 1910 until 1939, like myself, had a job for life. Starting with the engine, the main component was the crankcase which supported the twin flywheels attached to the crankshaft. Above the crankcase was the cylinder block in which the piston moved. Above the cylinder block was the cylinder head in which the combustion of fuel provided the energy to move the piston.

Turning now to the cream separator, the main frame is the centre portion to which the gearing is attached to drive the centrifuge at high speed to separate the cream from the whey. The motive power in this case being provided by the diary worker turning the handle. In the early part of the last century and the end of the nineteenth century most farmers worldwide used a Lister cream separator, making their own butter and cheese with the cream and selling the whey or separated milk to local families.

The picture features seventeen middle-aged and older foundrymen. When I write down my comments about them I am filled with nostalgia and have an uncanny feeling that they would be very pleased that after more than sixty years someone still remembers and admires them.

From the left in the back row is Frank Hicks who was in charge of production of all engine cylinders and cylinder blocks. Next is his brother Charlie Hicks who was coreshop foreman, then Jack Mansell, a skilled loose-pattern moulder, followed by George James with the same skills. Last is Jack Workman from the Patch, Slimbridge, who was in charge of cylinder-head production. First left in the second row is Tommy Lane a skilled coremaker also from Slimbridge. On his left is another skilled coremaker

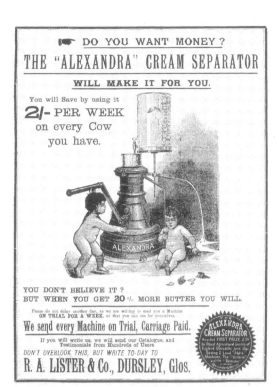

An advertisement for the Alexandra Cream Separator as it appeared in *The Dursley Gazette* on 19 November 1892. (Courtesy David Evans; picture taken from his book *Mr Pedersen, A Man of Genius*)

Mikael and Dagmar Pedersen in 1898. The cycle she is riding is a small men's, though at first called a lady's, and she is wearing a divided skirt. Such garments proved not to be popular with women and so to cater for them, Mikael designed a drop-frame machine. (Courtesy David Evans; picture taken from his book *Mr Pedersen, A Man of Genius*)

Harry Phillips, then Bill Atkins another skilled coremaker. On his left is Bert Cane, a skilled moulder who produced the large engine bedplates. Next to Bert is Harry Brown who was about to retire and was the pattern storekeeper. First left in the bottom row is Frank Griffin who was responsible for cream-separator main frames. On Frank's left is Tommy Blunsden from Waterley Bottom, his responsibility was the crankcase for the 5hp diesel engine. Next is Freddie Fryer from Rowley Cam. He was a super craftsman and produced the double-sided pattern plates used by the plate moulders from an original wooden mater pattern. The foundry manager, Mr Charlie Smith, wearing a suit, tie and trilby hat is sitting on Freddie's left. He was a well-respected craftsman and strict disciplinarian. On Mr Smith's left is Joe Sutton who was in charge of the production of crankcase castings for the JP range of engines.

These engines, the three and four-cylinder versions, were used coupled to Mawdsley generators mounted on trailers supplied by Taskers of Andover and were the sole sources of energy for the Second World War mobile searchlight and radar units. On Joe's left is Bill Ford who fettled the crankcases made by Joe. Last in the bottom row is Jim Harris who made the cast-iron pistons then used in some Lister engines. To end I want to record that the War Dept had one of its senior inspectors permanently based in the works during the Second World War. He was Bill Clark, a good friend, who lived at Costwold Green in Stonehouse. Bill's wife was deputy head at the Girls' Central School at Downfield before it merged with the Girls' High School.

CREAM OF LISTER'S WORKFORCE

My intention here is to record memories of Lister's cream-separating apparatus, an unusual bicycle and the engineer who designed them both.

Mikael Pedersen, a Dane, was employed by Sir Ashton Lister to develop cream-separating equipment which he did successfully. It involved using a centrifugal force. Milk was poured into a bowl rotating at high speed and it formed two layers. The heavier whey was drained off via one spout while the lighter cream was drained off by another.

Pedersen was also responsible for the design and development of an unusual 'safety bicycle' which was an improvement on the Penny Farthing Bicycle in common use at the time. I find it difficult to describe, but the bike involved a triangular frame with a saddle in the form of a hammock rather than the leather saddle used on Penny Farthings. The bicycles were made in what was previously a cloth mill driven by a water wheel using the Broadwell Spring. This building was known as Howard's Upper Mill.

Dursley Pedersen bicycles were produced in this mill until the beginning of the First World War in 1914, after which production ceased and the mill was no longer used for that purpose.

When I joined the company in 1931, the main ground-floor room of the mill was used as the Lister workers' mess room or canteen and half of the basement was used to store wooden patterns used for prototype engine and cream separators as well as for jigs and fixtures for production machining of components. The pattern-store keeper was Harry Brown who was nearing retirement and had been one of Sir Ashton Lister's original workers in the 1870s. Harry had been a skilled foundry craftsman but was physically incapable of carrying on with his normal job. He also had very bad eyesight and had been given the pattern store-keeper's job on compassionate grounds.

The wooden patterns and coreboxes (cores from the inside of castings) were piled up on the flagstone floor and the records written in pencil in a notebook. Poor old Harry very often took hours to find a pattern mainly because he could not read the pattern number which was impressed on an aluminium strip nailed on to the pattern with panel pins.

My superior at that time, Parnal Vigar, arranged for the foreman carpenter, Frank Owen, to have a wooden racking frame with shelves and cubicles to which I allocated letters from floor to ceiling and numbers horizontally from side to side. At the same time, Frank Owen had a card-index box made and, over quite a long period of time, we sorted out the patterns in numerical order and recorded their location in their respective cubicles on cards. This index system solved the problem and patterns could be found in minutes rather than hours.

I continued to help Harry when needed until his retirement, when he was replaced by Bill Huntingdon (Cockney Bill), an ex-soldier originally from London. Cockney Bill was very competent and developed the card-index system and a storage facility

Les with the model Lister engine. (Courtesy *Stroud News & Journal*)

The demolition of the R.A. Lister factory in 2002. (Courtesy Dr Ray Wilson of the Gloucestershire Society for Industrial Archaeology)

COAL WAS TOO DEAR FOR POOR FAMILIES

Mr L.E. Beard, a very popular, compassionate and ingenious local man known to everyone as 'Eddie', took over Eastington Coal Wharf, renting it from the Canal Co.

Eddie and his wife were personal friends of my father and mother and I used to spend a lot of time at his wharf with them.

I think that Eddie obtained his coal from Coppice Colliery and hired a narrow boat, but being a go-ahead man he dispensed with the horse and cart and purchased the first solid-tyred model T Ford lorry in the district.

The mid-1920s were a time of industrial unrest; unemployment was at an all-time high, wages were low and many families were so poor they could buy food but could not afford coal for heating and cooking. Eddie realised this and, as wood was plentiful and cheap, he bought a second-hand circular-saw bench and used a flat leather belt driven by one of the wheels of the jacked-up lorry to drive the saw. The belt was repeatedly coming off, but as the demand for cheap wood was increasing

Eddie bought himself a single cylinder L-type tank cooled Lister petrol engine. Lister engineers set up the engine and saw bench and soon Eddie had more than enough logs to satisfy his customers.   This was one of the last L-type petrol engines sold by the company which replaced it with the 5-1 diesel engine in 1930. The '5' indicated the horse power and the '1' indicated single cylinder. This wonderful engine was in production until the 1980s. At Lister's it was always known as 'Vive Oss', this being colloquial Gloucestershire for five horse power.

It was my privilege to have worked for R.A. Lister Ltd of Dursley as a foundry man for forty-nine years and to have been associated with this particular engine. I think I am the only surviving member of a team of engineers, nominated by the directors in the 1950s who were instructed to carry out on-going detailed research into manufacturing processes and component design to ensure that the engine remained the most reliable and gave better value for money than any of its competitors. The fact that 90 per cent of the components were made of cast iron meant that my involvement as a foundry man was greater than most. This fact was acknowledged by the directors of the company, then part of the Hawker Siddeley Group, and on my retirement on 23 July 1980 I was presented with a true-to-scale wooden model of the latest design of this engine. The model, which I think is unique and could be the only one in existence, is now with the Stroud Museum in the Park for safe keeping.

At this stage I should mention that Eddie Beard's L-Type petrol engine had twin six-spoked fly-wheels of about the same weight, whereas the engine used for Lister Bruston electricity generating sets carried about two heavy flywheels about twice the weight. The increased inertia ensured that the power output remained constant. The heavy flywheels were chosen for the model because the six-spoked flywheels would have been very fragile when made in wood.

On Thursday 30 September 2001 it was my pleasure to be taken by the very professional *Stroud News & Journal* photographer, Mark Watkins, to the Museum in the Park, where he took a picture of me holding the model engine. I realise I have been describing the model as that of a 5hp single cylinder engine whereas, through continuous research and development, its power output was increased to 8hp and I should have called it an 8-1 rather than a 5-1. Please accept my apologies for that error (old age must be beginning to get to me!).

While I am a regular visitor to the old museum in Lansdown, this was the very first time I had visited the very up-to-date Museum in the Park. It is a museum to be proud of with very knowledgeable and attentive staff. If anyone who chooses to read this and is interested in Stroud district's past they will find that a visit to the new museum is most interesting and rewarding.

To conclude this article I would like to pay tribute to the workers at the now closed Cinderford factory of R.A. Lister & Co. Ltd who were the last to produce this engine. They were the most industrious workers I have known and maintained a very high production rate and quality standard. I speak with some knowledge as I paid weekly visits to the factory in a technical liaison capacity with the late Roy Werrett, the group quality control manager.

R.A. Lister new foundry building just after it was opened in 1939. (Courtesy Andrew Bar

Weavers at Lodgemoor Cloth Mills, 1912. Winifred Davis is pictured far right.

Looking Back to Times at the Mill

This very short bit of nostalgia features postcards produced around 1913-14. They are pictures of the female and male employees of Lodgemore Mill.

My wife Peggy's mother is on the extreme right of the one taken of the weavers (see picture above) all of whom are wearing spotless white dresses. Her name was Winifred Davis; she lived at Ruscombe and walked to and from work at Lodgemore Mill. Shortly after this photograph was taken at the beginning of the First World War, George volunteered to join the Army and became a private in the Gloucestershire Regiment.

Winifred told me that George would 'tune', that is 'set up' the Huddersfield-made Dobcross looms which she operated and that she personally wove the broadcloth destined to become the world of famous scarlet tunics worn by guards' officers. The scarlet dye used was made with natural ingredients by the Young family who had a dye works adjacent to Lower Mills at Bridgend in Stonehouse. She alleged that the formula for the scarlet dye was never written down but passed down through generation of the Young family.

I was born in a cottage owned by Whitminster House which was near the site of the Whitminster Mill on 8 August 1915. There was no evidence of the mill's existence, it being one of the first to be demolished.

From Whitminster the next mill is the Fromebridge Mill. This, thankfully, has been preserved and is now a sumptuous up-market and very popular restaurant. As a small boy I was well acquainted with Fromebridge Mill because every autumn my father used to take his apples and pears by horse and cart to the mill. The apples would be made into cider and the pears into perry. Both were the favourite drinks of country people in the early 1900s.

I now want to quote from Dr Stephen Mills' article 'Fromebridge Mill, Frampton-on-Severn' which appeared in the *Gloucestershire Society for Industrial Archaeology (GSIA) Journal* (1988):

> Frombridge can claim a history as long and as complex as any in the area. It was recorded in the Domesday survey as a corn mill.
>
> In 1350 it had been partially converted for 'fulling' cloth. In 1498 it was a 'corn malt and fulling' mill. Its use for fulling cloth ceased in 1632 and three corn mills were sold. In 1713 the site comprised of four corn mills.
>
> In 1760 it ceased to be a complex of corn mills and was converted to a substantial iron and wire works known as the Frombridge Company and was part of the Purnell family empire.
>
> The wire was used in the manufacture of 'cards' for the woollen industry as well as being supplied for fish hooks for the Newfoundland fisheries. It is also recorded that there must have been a brass foundry there as brass wire brass pins were being produced.

At this stage I must end this rewarding dip into the local history of times long past and extend my personal thanks to the organisation which has retained much of the original building which may be as much as 800 years old.

THE ART OF SELLING FISH ON A GRAND SCALE

Jim Ball, a small but witty man with a very loud voice, was a fishmonger and fish hawker in the Stroud district, a very welcome annual visitor to Dursley in the 1930s.

On the Wednesday before Good Friday he would put up posters at various locations in the Dursley streets. They would read: 'Jim Ball the fish King coming tonight.' Very early, between 4-5 a.m. the Thursday before Good Friday, he would transport trestle tables and dozens of boxes containing wet fish packed in ice to the Market House. He would set up these tables covered by boxes of fish, with many more waiting on the floor. He would have all this ready before the Lister workers began to come to work between 7- 7.30 a.m.

In those far-off days the individuals who hawked their wares and specific 'cries' similar to those of the present-day town criers. Some that I can well remember were 'fishy' Webb, a lady fish hawker who lived at the bottom of Whitminster Pitch on the A38 Bristol Road. She drove a pony and trap and her cry was 'Fish O, Fish O.'

Another was 'Raggy' Smith who lived in a cottage at Stanley Downton, near Stonehouse. In the 1920s I remember him pushing an old 'pram' and crying: 'Rag bones, rag bones.' In fact, he was known as the 'rag and bone man' and was always smoking a very short clay pipe which was known as a 'nose warmer'.

To return to Jim Ball, he was quite articulate and would engage in banter with the passers-by. He had some unique descriptions of fish, most memorable being cod's roe as 'iddly-diddly' fish.

The Lister workers, especially those in the iron foundry in which I worked, really welcomed Jim Ball as bargains were to be had. One of those workers was 'Bronco' Bailey (real name Bill), who came from Wotton-under-Edge, and was one of about twenty plate moulders who were the quantity producers of the smaller iron castings before the advent of mechanisation.

In those days, Lister's were just coming out of the industrial depression which followed the 1926 General Strike, the plate moulders were happy to have a job and wages and sang as they worked, especially at Christmas time.

Bronco usually started the singing, but on the Wednesday before Good Friday he would spend most of the morning crying out: 'Jim Ball the Fish King coming tonight,' much to the amusement of his fellow workers. During the 12 noon to 1 p.m. lunch hour hordes of Lister workers would rush up Long Street to the Market House to purchase the very popular 'iddly-diddly' fish before they were all sold.

A Story behind Every Nickname

The dictionary defines a nickname as 'a name added to or substituted for a regular name.' In the early part of the last century nicknames were used to a much greater extent than they are today. In fact casual acquaintances were often known only by their nickname. I can recall many nicknames in common use in the 1930s, some of which by today's standards would be unfit for publication. However, I have chosen a few of those used in the R.A. Lister Iron Foundry at that time. Stroud people were always called Stroudies and those from Chippenham, Chippies. Gloucester residents were called Spotties, presumably after the Gloucester Old Spot Pig. To have been born in the Forest of Dean, especially Ruardean, would attract the nickname Bear.

While most name calling was taken in good grace it was known that Foresters were very sensitive to the often repeated question 'who killed the bear?' and it was not unknown for a fight to start between the persistent name caller and the Forester. However, this would soon be over and they would be the best of friends. Old Butties again, as the Forester would describe it. If asked who started the fight the Forester's reply would be ''im did'.

Moving nearer to Dursley, it was the people living in Nympsfield who were subject to most leg pulling and name calling. Nympy as it was always called, was then so isolated that its inhabitants were always considered to be a little bit eccentric. It was alleged that one local inhabitant put his pig on a wall to see a brass band pass by.

This little ditty was often repeated in jest when leg-pulling was taking place:

Nympy is a funny place, stands upon a tump,
Everybody there eats ag-pag dump.

To explain, ag-pags were sloes and dump was a pudding. It also explains why Nympsfield residents were known as ag-pags.

Those living in the Parish of Coaley were always known as Coaley Crows and very often the younger element would approach a local flapping their arms and calling out 'caw caw'. Before concluding this trip a very long way down memory lane, I feel that I must mention a few nicknames of some of my long-time friends. Sadly, most are no longer with us.

To commence, Charlie Smith, the foreman of the iron foundry was Father. Frank Hicks was Hooky beak as he had an aquiline nose, his brother Charlie was Ticker. George Evans was Trample Daisy, he had very large feet. Jim Freeman from Nympy was Burglar and Charlie was Bang Bang. Bill Atkins from Rowley in Cam was Bottler, he used to fetch bottles of drinking water from the Broadwell springs when he was much younger. Bill Law of Frampton was Bonar after the politician of that name. Bill Bailey of Synwell, Wotton-under-Edge, was Broncho. Alf Pearce from Coaley was Dusty. Bill Price from Dursley was Bladder Head. Ted Joyner from Gloucester was Spottie. Ron Morse of Ruardean was the Bear. Charlie Arnold of Ebley was Bottle Ass (he had a large posterior). Hubert Samuel from Wales was The Square Man and Vincent Thomas from Horsley was Mussolini.

REMEMBERING THE DAYS WHEN MOLESKIN WAS CONSIDERABLY VALUABLE

In the 1700 and 1800s and the Industrial Revolution, the British Iron Foundry industry was the foundation on which that revolution was built. Cast iron was the material which was used for every conceivable item from the humble 'flat iron' used to 'iron' washing to ships, bridges, textile and agricultural implements, steam engines, fireplaces, cooking ranges (AGA still use it), saucepans and frying pans etc (Le Creuset still use it) and later petrol and diesel engines. All of these items were produced by 'iron moulders' who had to serve a seven-year indentured apprenticeship before they could claim a 'skilled man' status. These iron moulders who spent most of their time kneeling on the damp sand of the foundry floor or 'turf' which was the description accepted by all true foundrymen.

They all wore trousers made of moleskins. This was a 'cottage industry' and moleskin trouser makers existed in most areas. The trousers were made to measure with the fur on the inside of the trousers. They were damp proof and would not ignite if splashes of molten iron came into contact with them. They were never washed and the skins were sewn together using a waxed cord or thin string. This was known as 'wax end' and was also used by boot, shoe and leather 'legging' makers. They would last for years and could be repaired if the splashes of molten iron had burnt away the stitches.

When I was very young living at Westend in Eastington, my father would set traps to catch moles. The traps were in the form of a pair of spring-loaded twin-curved 'scissors' with a device which kept the twin scissors open and would be set under the 'mole heave' which was the name of the pile of earth pushed up by the mole as he burrowed his way in search of worms. The mole, whose eyesight was bad, would push against the device as he travelled along his run, this would release the device which released the twin-curved scissors to catch the mole without damaging the skin. The traps would be left 'in situ' until the part of the scissors above ground were seen to be open which indicated that the trap had been sprung and a mole caught. My father would skin the mole and nail the skin to a board. The skins were allowed to dry naturally and the carcasses thrown down to be picked up by carrion crows who knew that an easy meal was to be had. The dried skins would be kept until the itinerant mole catcher came to collect them. He paid 2d for each skin. Sometimes my father had twenty to thirty dried skins to sell.

3

WAR

POIGNANT WARTIME MEMORIES

To start this latest trip down memory lane I feel that the exhibition of documents and artefacts relating to those horrendous wartime years would serve to illustrate some of the differences between those years of deprivation and the peace and affluence most of us enjoy today.

The card which the majority of R.A. Lister employees received; it shows that before the war had started, they had volunteered to become blood donors.

The Works Pass No. 57, issued to me on 21 March 1942. It features a photograph of a very young Les Pugh – I was twenty-six and my national identity number ODRA Y6/1. Uniformed security guards were on duty twenty-four hours a day, seven days a week, and no one was admitted to the works until the guards had checked the pass.

The photograph taken by Mr E.C. Peckham of Stroud. It features the Stonehouse Platoon E Company, 8th Gloucestershire Battalion of the Home Guard Regiment. The Home Guard Regiment was originally the Local Defence Volunteers force, which was hurriedly formed after the evacuation of the BEF from Dunkirk in the mid-1940s to assist what was left of the British Army when German invasion of Britain was considered to be imminent. As members of the LDV all we had was a khaki armband with the letters LDV printed on it in black. We had no weapons other than shot guns except that officers from the First World War still had their revolvers. After a relatively short period it was announced that the LDV would in future be known as the Home Guard Regiment and that full regulation battle dress and kit would be issued. This included a Forage Cap with the Gloucester's Regimental badge and back badge which is unique in the Gloucestershire Regiment and of which we were immensely proud.

Also shown are photographs of my Certificate of Proficiency Home Guard (see page 62), dated 7 March 1944, when I was promoted to the rank of Lance Corporal

This is to certify that

Mr Leslie Charles Pugh

volunteered as a Donor of Blood
under the R. A. Lister Wartime
Emergency Service Scheme.

p.p. R. A. Lister & Co. Ltd.

Sept. 1st. 1939

Kiel

Secretary.

Les's Blood Donor Card.

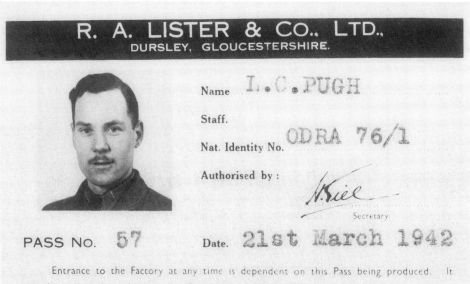

R. A. LISTER & CO., LTD.,
DURSLEY, GLOUCESTERSHIRE.

Name L. C. PUGH

Staff.

Nat. Identity No. ODRA 76/1

Authorised by :

Kiel

Secretary.

PASS No. 57   Date. 21st March 1942

Entrance to the Factory at any time is dependent on this Pass being produced. It must be returned on leaving the Company's employment, and if lost, the fact must be reported immediately to the Employment Office. New Passes will be charged for at cost.

FINDER PLEASE FORWARD TO POLICE STATION.

R. A. Lister's Works' Pass.

Stonehouse Platoon Home Guard, the VE celebrations, Stroud, 1945 Les is standing third from left, back row. (Courtesy Peckham's, Stroud)

Bridgend Hostel, 1943. (Courtesy Esther Carnell)

and the citation given to all Home Guard personnel giving their name and length of service, which in my case was 23 June 1940-31 December 1944.

The standing down of the Home Guard on 31 December 1944 was the first indication that the Allies were winning the war in Europe. The events leading to victory in Europe started in January 1944 when the 1,000-day siege of Leningrad ended. In March the retreating Germans entered Hungary at the same time that the Allies bombed Nuremberg In May Allied forces gathered in Britain for the invasion of Europe. In June Allied forces invaded German-occupied France. In the same month V-1 rockets were launched against Britain. In September Allied troops liberated Paris and the first German V2 rockets hit Britain. In December, Germany made the last counter attack in the Ardennes Forest. In January 1945, the Red Army liberated Warsaw and entered German territory. In February the Allies bombed Dresden.

In March the Allies crossed the Rhine into Germany. In April American and Soviet troops met on the River Elbe. Mussolini was captured by Italian partisans and shot.

Hitler committed suicide in his underground bunker. On 8 May Germany surrendered and VE Day was declared. Spontaneous celebrations took place on the streets of Stroud and similar celebrations were held in Stonehouse with a bonfire on Doverow Hill.

The History of the Bridgend Hostel

There is little doubt that Bridgend has housed more nationalities than any other part of Gloucestershire. The Bridgend Hostel was built on green fields in 1942-1943 to accommodate hundreds of young female workers who were drafted from the West Country to work in the Sperry Gyroscope and Hoffman Bearings factories. Both companies had moved from the London area to the relative safety of rural Stonehouse.

I am fortunate to know two women who worked on the domestic staff at the hostel, who were Esther Carnell from Newton Abbot in Devon and Dora Lambert from Sheepscombe. These are the names by which they were known when they worked at the hostel.

Esther has written a letter to me which reads:

I left Newton Abbot for Stonehouse in March 1943 when I was 21. I went to work as a domestic at the hostel in Bridgend Estate. The hostel housed some of the girls who worked in the Hoffman and Sperry factories. My job was to look after their rooms, make the beds, clean and dust, etc. I looked after two blocks and worked from 8am to 5pm, having a break at lunchtime. Sometimes I had to work in the evenings because the girls on night work were sleeping by day. So I had to do their rooms later.

We had one day off a week, and often two of us would catch the bus to places like Gloucester and Cheltenham. Sometimes we would go by bus to Nailsworth and walk back over Rodborough Common to Stroud, calling in at the Bear Inn for afternoon tea.

We had our meals in a large canteen which was cleaned on a Saturday night when the American soldiers from a nearby base would come with their band for a dance.

The domestic staff at Bridgend Hostel. (Courtesy Esther Carnell)

The domestic staff in the canteen at Bridgend Hostel. (Courtesy Esther Carnell)

Dora Lambert with her dog.

Esther and Kathleen. The Stonehouse Paper Bag Factory in the background was still operating in 2008.

This ends Esther's letter. I would add a good time was had by all.

To end this small portion of social history I would add that when the war ended in 1945 the female workers went back to their homes and the hostel was used to house men from Eastern Europe who chose to remain in England. Most were Polish ex-service men, who with many of their fellow countrymen had previously been housed at camps at Babdown near Tetbury and Daglingworth near Cirencester. Up to 700 of these workers were engaged by ex-Polish army officer W.J. (George) Kucjuk who was liaison officer to Sam Marshall, (R.A. Lister's employment officer), to work in Lister's Dursley factory. A large percentage came to work in the company's iron foundry which was then the most modern in Europe.

At that time I was a foreman and I had the responsibility for teaching them the necessary skills they would need as semi-skilled foundry operatives. They were anxious to learn and I derived considerable satisfaction for being able to help them. I also appreciated the respect that was shown to me as their instructor. Like myself they will now be very old men, if they are still alive.

READY TO PROTECT HIS COUNTRY WITH HIS LIFE

Soon after the evacuation of the BEF from Dunkirk, an appeal was made for all able-bodied men to join the Local Defence Volunteers to assist what was left of the Army. We were asked to report at the local police station.

Certificate of Proficiency
HOME GUARD

On arrival at the Training Establishment, Primary Training Centre or Recruit Training Centre, the holder must produce this Certificate at once for the officer commanding, together with Certificate A if gained in the Junior Training Corps or Army Cadet Force.

PART I. I hereby certify that (Rank) L/Cpl. (Name and initials) Pugh, L.S. of 'E' ~~Battery~~ Company 8 Glos H.G. ~~Regiment~~ Battalion HOME GUARD has qualified in the Proficiency Badge tests as laid down in the pamphlet "Qualifications for, and Conditions governing the Award of the Home Guard Proficiency Badges and Certificates" for the following subjects :—

	Subject	Date	Initials
1.	General knowledge (all candidates)	5ᵗ knowledge	
2.	Rifle		
3.	36 M Grenade		
4.	(a) Other weapon STEN		
	(b) Signalling		
5.	(a) Battlecraft, ~~(b) Coast Artillery, (c) Heavy A.A. Bty. work, (d) "Z" A.A. Battery work, (e) Bomb Disposal, (f) Watermanship, (g) M.T.~~	5.3.44.	A.R.J
6.	(a) Map Reading, ~~(b) Field works,~~ (c) ~~First Aid~~	5.3.44	B.H.J

Date 5ᵗ March 194 4   Signature H. R. Hedes. Maj
* President or Member of the Board.

Date 194   Signature
* President or Member of the Board.

Date 194   Signature
* President or Member of the Board.

Date 194   Signature
* President or Member of the Board.

Date 194   Signature
* President or Member of the Board.

PART II. I certify that (Rank) L/Cpl (Name and initials) Pugh, L.S. of 'E' ~~Battery~~ Company 8 Glos HG ~~Regiment~~ Battalion HOME GUARD, having duly passed the Proficiency tests in the subjects detailed above in accordance with the pamphlet and is hereby authorized to wear the Proficiency Badge as laid down in Regulations for the Home Guard, Vol. 1, 1942, para. 41d.

Date 7 March 1944   Signature
Commanding 8 Glos Bn. H.G.

PART III. If the holder joins H.M. Forces, his Company or equivalent Commander will record below any particulars which he considers useful in assessing the man's value on arrival at the T.E., P.T.C., R.T.C., e.g. service, rank, duties on which employed, power of leadership, etc.

Date 194   Signature
* Delete where not applicable.   O.C.

Home Guard Certificate of Proficiency, 7 March 1944.

In the years when our Country

was in mortal danger

LESLIE CHARLES PUGH

who served 23 July 1940 – 31 December 1944

gave generously of his time and

powers to make himself ready

for her defence by force of arms

and with his life if need be.

George R.I.

THE HOME GUARD

Les's certificate for serving in The Home Guard.

I went to Stonehouse Police Station on 13 July 1940 when about twenty of us signed on. Most were veterans of the First World War aged between fifty and sixty with three or four younger men like myself. I was twenty-five and working in what had previously been designated as a reserved occupation.

I had worked in the iron foundry of R.A. Lister & Co. Ltd of Dursley since leaving Marling School in 1931 and all skilled foundrymen were classified as essential to the war effort.

About a week after reporting to the police station we were contacted individually by the ex-officers and NCOs and asked to report to the Stonehouse Subscription Rooms. We were issued with a khaki armband on which the letters LDV had been printed in black. We were also asked to bring along any weapons that we might possess.

A few brought shotguns; otherwise we were completely unarmed. The ex-officers and NCOs took their normal rank and gave us some idea of what would be expected of us. While we were all enthusiastic, we knew that we would be no match for trained German paratroopers if they landed and naturally were very apprehensive.

From then on we assembled at the Sub Rooms one evening per week and Sunday mornings where we were drilled and exercised. After a few weeks a consignment of First World War Canadian Ross rifles arrived together with about fifty rounds of ammunition. From then on arms drill was the order of the day. An announcement was later made that the LDV would in future be known as the Home Guard and regulation battledress and kit would be issued. A month later we were issued with a battledress tunic, great coat, forage cap, black army boots, leather leggings, a steel helmet and regulation army gas mask. We were told we would be known as the Stonehouse Platoon of 'E' Company of the 8th Gloucestershire Regimental Badges. At last we felt that we were real soldiers. Training was dramatically stepped up and our platoon trainer was ex-Grenadier Guards Regimental Sergeant Major Charlie Williams of Stonehouse. One of many platoon commanders was Captain S.G. Annis, known as Titch, a strict disciplinarian.

With the permission of the Stonehouse Brick & Tile Co. we built a firing range in a disused section of the clay pit and had target practice about once a month. We were ordered to provide a nightly guard on the LMS railway viaduct at Beard's Mill. We had regular training exercises involving the whole of 'E' company. These were held in Woodchester Park near Nympsfield and involved the use of live hand grenades, known to us as 'Mills Bombs'.

A further exercise involving the Stonehouse platoon was a mock attack on the Sperry Gyroscope Co. at Bonds Mill. Sperry's had their own platoon and a Lewis machine gun mounted on the top of the security building. We were told to act as though we were German paratroops seeking to capture and destroy the factory. We reported back to our CO that the factory was well guarded and that there was no way that we could surprise them.

However, we thought that we could penetrate their defences by wading through the culvert which took the River Frome under the railway line. Cyril Baker and I volunteered. Being young and active I led the way, only to find that Sperry's had the culvert entrance under surveillance. By that time it was getting light so the operation was called off and I returned home like a drowned rat much to the annoyance of my wife who had the unenviable task of drying my battledress uniform.

Our next task was to provide a night guard on Stanley Mill which had been taken over by the Royal Navy as a safe store for vital equipment. By this time we were well equipped with Sten guns and one high-velocity Browning automatic rifle. I was put in charge of this weapon and given detailed instructions about its use and maintenance by a senior NCO. I also took a proficiency test and other disciplines and was given a Certificate of Proficiency and was promoted to the exalted rank of Lance Corporal. My certificate was dated 7 March 1944 – only nine months away from 31 December when the Home Guard was officially disbanded.

Early in 1945, all ex-Home Guard personnel received a letter through the post signed by King George VI. Mine read:

> In the years when our country was in mortal danger Leslie Charles Pugh, who served, July 23, 1940 – December 31, 1944, gave generously of his time and powers to make himself ready for her defence by force of arms and with his life if need be.

It is a sobering thought that probably less than five per cent of the Home Guard members who were privileged to serve their country when it was in mortal danger still survive. I feel certain that those few of us still feel the same sense of patriotism for our country that we did in the dark days of war all those years ago.

WAR BABY THAT BROUGHT US JOY

This is an article which is so personal that, until now, I have never considered writing it. However, the desperate shortage of foster parents to look after and care for unwanted or disadvantaged children, has reached crisis point. I am therefore quoting how my late wife Peggy and I were able to help an unwanted baby boy to enjoy the love and care that comes with living in a stable home environment. To do this I shall have to take you back more than seventy years to the 1930s. In that period it became obvious that Adolf Hitler was rearming and that war would be the inevitable consequence.

The British government of the day was aware of this and plans were made to evacuate a section of the Air Ministry from London to the relative safety of Wycliffe College. To do this, pupils and staff would be moved to Lampeter in mid-Wales to prearranged accommodation. Before the evacuation to Lampeter had started, the Air Ministry had notices printed in local newspapers asking for home owners in the district to provide furnished, rented accommodation for their executives who were coming to Stonehouse.

This would be for the duration of the war.

Peggy's mother, who was a First World War widow and a state-registered foster mother, had just had a detached house built in Field Road, Whiteshill, in which she lived and fostered an unwanted three-year-old girl. Peggy and her mother, wishing to help their country in time of need and with my wholehearted agreement, decided that the furnished house, Trevona, in Whiteshill, should be offered to the Air Ministry and that mother and foster girl would live with us in our new three-bedroom house at Bridgend, Stonehouse, in which I still live.

The Air Ministry gratefully accepted the offer and a lovely couple, Mr and Mrs Roland Hill, who were Air Ministry executives, took up residence. Peggy's mother and the foster girl came to live with us at Bridgend. A few months after moving to Bridgend, the little girl was formally adopted and two evacuees from the East End of London were billeted with us on the understanding that if a foster mother was urgently needed, they would be moved.

In late 1941, Joan Escort, the lady responsible for placing foster children, urgently needed a foster home for an as yet unborn and unwanted baby. She had advised the authorities and Peggy's mother about this and, as agreed, the evacuees were moved to another location.

On 18 December 1941, a ten-day-old baby boy called Michael was brought by Miss Escort and placed in a cot underneath the window of our dining room, which was the only warm room in the house. Fuel, both wood and coal, were in very short supply and no house had more than one fire. Peggy was delighted about the arrangements and, as we were both working, her mother looked after him, cooked our meals and did the housework.

From the moment he came, Peggy and I treated him as our own son, as, at that time, we had no children. We bought a new pram and all the necessary baby clothes. As he grew older I made wooden toys for him. There was a shortage of everything and food was rationed. When he attained school age, Peggy took him to Stonehouse Primary School from where he moved to the Boys' Central School at Downfield. On leaving Central I arranged for him to take an indentured apprenticeship with a local engineering company and to attend the Stroud Technical College. He left as a qualified engineer, had regular employment, married, had children and now grandchildren. It is my wish that he should remain anonymous, so I don't want to reveal his surname.

The pleasure and satisfaction that my late wife Peggy and myself obtained from our decision to be his foster parents by proxy was so great that I have no words to describe it.

Chocolate was a Rare Treat

Before I relate the memories of Judi Fitzpatrick (née Lewis), the evacuee who stayed with us during the Second World War, I would like to say thank you to Mary Richards of Nympsfield who wrote me a delightful letter which solved a mystery. I have always wondered why her uncle, Jim Freeman, was called 'Burglar'. Mary wrote: 'Jim Freeman was called burglar because he played the role of a robber in one of Nympy's plays,' presumably while still at school.

Mary also wrote that Jim Harris, who lost his eye in a terrible accident in R.A. Lister's Dursley foundry, was a great friend of her dad, Jack Freeman, who was a skilled coremaker and a very valued member of the foundry team.

Now to continue with Judi's wonderful letter. She wrote:

Things were viewed by us children in a different light and were quite exciting to us back then (such as discovering a patch of four-leaved clover). I still have one or two which I pressed in a book, though where it is at the moment I don't know.

Another nice way of whiling away a day was to go to the various streams and woodlands to look at the wildlife. We were only taken by a teacher to catch minnows in jam jars and also to catch sticklebacks to take back to the classroom.

Another thing I remember was the shortage of chocolates and sweets. When the sweet shop got some in, the word would go round and we would all take turns to go into the shop, asking if they had any chocolate.

Sometimes we would be sent packing and other times would be allowed to spend our pocket money on maybe a bar of chocolate – then if only one was available we would all pay or trade for a share. It seems incredible now when you look around and see children gobbling down chocolate, sweets, crisps and ice creams etc. I wonder how they would fare on wartime rations.

Another highlight, rare but very clearly remembered, was a trip to town. I can't remember what it looked like, but it always seemed to be a great adventure and treat to go. On one occasion, three or four of us were invited to go and play and then be given tea with a girl who had a very rich family and lived in a big house.

The girl was so spoiled every time any one of us tried to play with any of her toys she screamed for her mother and we were told not to touch her things. We were given tea later which was very nice with cakes and other things, but we all decided even for the free tea it was not worth going again.

Judy Pays for Dreaming

Judy writes:

There were one or two unpleasant memories including being sent to a hairdressers who charged 2s, then when it needed cutting again she charged 2s 6d.

When I told Mrs Keen [Peggy's mother who was living with us] she sent me back to get the 6d overcharge probably because she thought I had spent it. The hairdresser was a bit bemused, no one had ever done that before, but seeing that I was upset about it, she gave me back 6d.

I was also accused, unfairly, of stealing the milk money returns. We paid 6d a week for milk for five mornings. Sometimes the cows didn't produce enough so if we missed two days we would be given 1d back to take to our mothers or carers. Being a bit of a dreamer, I would put it in my pocket and then promptly forget what it was. When I found it in my pocket at a later date I would think I was rich and that it must be some pocket money I had overlooked and would promptly spend it.

I was also hauled before the headmaster and accused of stealing. I think he knew I hadn't meant to steal, but he tried to find out what had happened. I was too frightened and overawed at the enormity of being summoned in front of the whole school to explain myself that I just said 'yes' to everything.

Later, after leaving Stonehouse, I was sent to a convent school for girls where I managed to catch up on my schooling and actually learned something for once.

When I left school at fifteen I was apprenticed to Heal & Son Ltd, furniture makers and bedding specialists in Tottenham Court Road, W1, for three years. I got married at nineteen and left Heals for two years but went back after my marriage failed and stayed for fifteen years. I then remarried and retired from work to bring up our son Adam and later my stepson Graeme. I guess being an evacuee didn't really harm me in the long run.

Fate and War made us Friends

Earlier this year I sat in the front room of my house with Jan Sowa, known to everyone as Jack. Jack lives with his wife, Ray, at Bridgend, Stonehouse which is many hundreds of miles away from his birthplace of Tarnov in Poland. He was born on 9 July 1927. His father was a regular soldier in the Polish army and Jack attended school at neighbouring Stolpge.

On 1 September 1939 the Nazis invaded Poland from the west and soon after, the Russians invaded from the east. The brave Polish army soon fell and an 'every man for himself' situation followed. Jack's father hid in a wood but was soon found and taken prisoner.

Jack, his mother and brother, Ted, existed on soup and a few vegetables at home in intolerable conditions for seven months. One day the Nazis came, rounded up all the local families like cattle and put them on a freight train to Siberia where they stayed for two years in even more intolerable conditions. Jack was then fourteen years old. Their next move was to Ashcahbot near Tashkent. After one week Jack joined the 'young soldiers' who were all under sixteen. They attended a Palestine military school until he was nineteen. He was then demobilised and sent with his family to an army camp in East Anglia.

Jack's mother was later sent to Aberporth Camp in South Wales while Jack was sent to the Bridgend Hostel in Stonehouse which had been vacated by the female war workers at Sperrys and Hoffmans, for which it was built. Jack and Ted found work as labourers at Ham Mill Carpet factory at Thrupp. Jack left Ham Mill in 1951 to work for Hoffmans in its new hearing factory at Stonehouse. Both were still Polish citizens but after seven years they became naturalised British citizens, as did their mother. Also in 1951 Jack's mother bought a house in Downfield near Stroud and Jack and Ted went to live with her.

Jack met the love of his life, Ray Hughes at a dance held in Stonehouse Subscription Rooms which is now part of Wycliffe College. Ray and her family had left Bridgend in South Wales to live in the prefabricated bungalows near the Stroudwater Canal at Bridgend, Stonehouse, and to work at Hoffmans. Jack and Ray married, had one son, Michael, and went to live in Woodcock Lane, Stonehouse. These were also built to accommodate war workers.

When Jack was made redundant from Hoffmans in the early 1970s, he took a job at Daniel's Lightpill factory and subsequently at Fibrecrete at Chalford. He was unaware of the dangers of working with asbestos and his job involved handling the partly finished product in which the wet asbestos fibre sheets were corrugated.

Once again he was made redundant and he moved to R.A. Lister's factory in Dursley. Like myself, Jack found R.A. Lister to be an excellent employer and stayed there until he retired in 1992 at the age of sixty-five. He remembers with affection his foreman Mr Davies and his workmates in the engine stores who contributed generously to his retirement gifts.

Jack is a credit to his family, to Poland and to Britain. I am privileged to call him a friend.

Above: Egyptian exile Mrs Thorn who lived at Bridgend Hostel, standing in front of Les's Morris Minor which he bought in 1952

Left: Les's Ration Book.

MOST PEOPLE KNEW AN INVASION WAS IMMINENT

The D-Day landings on 6 June 1944 did not surprise many people in Gloucestershire. When the American troops came to the country in ever-increasing numbers we all knew the invasion of Europe by Allied forces was the ultimate objective. The cancellation of leave for all American forces indicated action was imminent.

On 6 June we left Stonehouse at 6.30 a.m. to arrive at R.A. Lister's Dursley factory to start work at 7.30 a.m. When we arrived at the Midland Railway Bridge over the A419 main road we met a convoy of American vehicles, jeeps, Dodge trucks and half-tracked vehicles loaded with American soldiers dressed in full battle order. The convoy, which had started from Frampton Green, was still coming up the A38 Bristol Road and into the A419 when we reached Claypits to turn left to Dursley. At the same time the air was full of Dakota twin-engined troop-carrying aircraft. All were flying towards the south coast.

We deduced that these forces which were assembled in Gloucestershire and Wiltshire would be the second contingent to cross the Channel after the vanguard had left the coastal area. While it is not relevant exclusively to the D-Day landings, the present generation should know that Lister three- and four-cylinder JP engines with Mawdsley dynamos mounted on the trailers, made by Taskers of Andover, were chosen by the War Dept to provide the energy used by searchlights, mobile radar equipment and mobile bakery units. The single-cylinder version of this engine, the 9-1, was used to power large numbers of landing craft used in the invasion.

The Lister Auto Truck was used to move equipment at military bases. Another use of Lister 'junior' petrol engines was to power the pumps on petrol bowsers or tankers from which both the fighting and transport vehicles were refuelled. We knew that as members of the Home Guard (Dad's Army) we would no longer be wanted. We were officially 'stood down' on 31 December 1944.

4

FESTIVITIES

JOHNNIE REVIVES MAY DAY

For this current nostalgic journey back to the early 1900s the memory concentrates on one subject, namely the May Day celebrations at Eastington C of E School and the man who made them happen, the late Revd J. W. Rowbotham, our beloved 'Johnnie'. If he were still alive he would be thrilled to hear himself called by his nickname. He was indeed a wonderful headmaster and devoted all his energies, not only to teaching, but also to the social aspect and he alone made the May Day celebrations a very important date.

Johnnie came to Eastington in 1906 and revived the May Day celebrations in 1907 which continued without a break until 1953. The May queen, elected by her fellow scholars, was crowned at the school before we marched around the parish followed by a crowd of parents and sightseers, with stops for maypole and Morris dancing, and for refreshments on resident's lawns.

In the first years a comb and tissue paper band headed the procession and provided accompaniment to the dancers. During the years when I was a pupil, 1920 to 1927, the comb band had been superseded by a kazoo band which were played by some of the older boys. Others carried the 'Hail to the May Queen' banner while the biggest and strongest carried the maypole and held it upright as the younger pupils danced. The May queen had four maids of honour and two page boys, also elected by fellow pupils. The crowning ceremony was carried out by Johnnie.

After this the first and most important visit was to the large house, the Leaze, now known as Eastington Park. It was the residence of the Bush family who were very wealthy and employed many domestic servants and outdoor staff. They were very generous too, and very interested in the school. They provided gifts for prize giving, a Christmas tree and presents at Christmas time as well as a donation on May Day.

Above and below: May Day celebrations at Eastington School, 1932. (Courtesy of Mrs Barnfield)

The next visit was to Oldbury House, now the Grange Nursing Home, which was occupied by the Capel family who were also very supportive of the school. From Oldbury House, we proceeded to Nupend Farm, then occupied by Mrs Reynolds, who always provided currant buns for all the children.

Our next call was to Eastington House, currently the home of Mr and Mrs Dick James, but it was then occupied by the Trower family.

From there we moved to the next house on the left-hand side of Springhill Pitch which was then Eastington Rectory, the home of the Revd George Thomas Attimus Ward, a great orator.

The next and last visit was to Alkerton Court, the home of Captain Turner, who again made a very generous donation. We then proceeded back to the school where the older boys helped to dismantle the stage and put away the maypole and banner for another year.

Magic of Christmas Never Diminishes

This bit of nostalgia is all about Christmas which was, and always will be a magical time of the year.

The first Christmas that I can remember distinctly is the one celebrated by my father Bill, my mother Florence, my brother Percy, who was ten years older than me, and myself. The year was 1920. I was five years old and had attended Eastington C of E School since September. We lived at Rose Cottage, Westend, Eastington, which was the last house in that parish with the boundary with Whitminster being a few yards further up Grove Lane.

The night before Christmas my father and mother went to midnight mass at Eastington Church, having put me to bed early leaving my brother in charge. Like all five-year-olds, I was wildly excited. I had hung my stockings on a chair near the mantelpiece in the front room which had an open fireplace which we rarely used. The staircase, which was open, was in the left-hand corner of the room next to the fireplace. This made the room very draughty and cold so it was never used in the winter. Nevertheless, Father Christmas always came down that chimney and filled my stockings with nuts and oranges in the bottom and small toys wrapped in Christmas paper to fill each stocking. He also left the *Playbox Annual* which my mother would read to me, a small mouth organ and a clockwork train set.

Incidentally, Christmas Day 1920 was on a Saturday. I know this because for many years I have owned a 100-year calendar for every day from 1891 to 1990. On the front cover is printed: 'Be careful for 100 years and you won't have to worry'.

Mr and Mrs George de Lisle Bush of the Leaze in Eastington School supplied a large Christmas tree every Christmas, grown on their estate, with real miniature candles in clip-on holders which were lit in the early afternoon on Christmas Eve when the school broke up for two weeks' holiday.

There was a present on the tree for every pupil. They also presented a book for each pupil who was top of each class in reading, writing and arithmetic. I remember that

I generally had the book for writing which was then known as composition. (As you know I still love writing and have to thank Miss Elsie Watts, the infants' teacher, for instilling that love.) The presents were distributed after we had sung Christmas carols which Mr and Mrs Bush really enjoyed.

Coronation Day

It was in the early 1920s when I recalled the pleasure I derived from my hobby of car spotting. This activity was the forerunner of another discipline, that of keeping a pocket diary. It is true to say that I was, still am and always will be an enthusiast.

On reflection I have to admit that a compulsive diarist would be a more accurate description. I cannot recall any instance since 1951 when I did not write up my diary at the end of each day. I even managed to do this after having major surgery (a loop ileostomy) for bowel cancer at Gloucester Royal Hospital on 16 October 2001, when I was eighty-six years old. I am now looking at my entry for that day and my writing is so bad that no one but me would be able to read it. Had I not had an epidural continuous injection into my spine to relieve the intense pain from the surgery, writing would have been impossible.

I was also able to write up my diary when the closure of the ileostomy was performed on 31 October 2001. This would be an opportune moment to say a big thank you to that wonderful consultant surgeon Mr W.H. Thomson and his team at Gloucester Royal Hospital. My thanks also the dedicated staff of Ward 9A and Ward 10. Collectively they saved my life.

Still on the same subject of keeping a diary, we have just celebrated the 50th anniversary of the crowning of Her Majesty Queen Elizabeth II on 2 July 1953. Reference to my diary for that year tells me that Coronation Day was dull and stormy with a cool wind. On Saturday 30 May, I decorated the front of our house with small Union Flags and fairy lights. On Sunday my wife Peggy and I attended a special Coronation evensong service at Cainscross Church at which I was a sidesman and member of the Parochial Church Council.

Monday 1 June was a national holiday and I drove our Clarendon grey 1951 Morris Minor LDG 499 to Cheltenham via Stroud so that the family could view the decorations.

On Coronation Day we watched the television broadcasts of the ceremony at our neighbour's house. They were Mr and Mrs Don Dunkason and daughter Glenis. They were one of very few families to own a television set. It had a 9in screen and the picture was a poor quality. After lunch we drove to Hoffman's sports' field where children's sports and a Punch and Judy show had been organised. At 9 p.m. we joined a torchlight procession to the top of Doverow Hill where a large bonfire was lit at 10 p.m.

Les aged twenty with his father Bill. (Courtesy *Stroud News & Journal*)

MEMORIES OF A ROYAL VISIT

Sixty-three years ago, on Maundy Thursday 1940, Queen Mary, who was staying at Badminton, paid a morale-boosting visit to the Stroud and Dursley district at very short notice. I have a very clear recollection of her visit to the Dursley Works of R.A. Lister and Co. Ltd.

Although every department made special preparation for her visit, the workers carried on with their allotted tasks in the normal efficient manner which was run by the five grandsons of the founder Sir Ashton Lister. Most had served as officers in the First World War and military-style discipline was enforced and accepted by the dedicated workforce who knew that, if they so desired, they had a job for life.

The Queen's visit to Lister's started at 3 p.m. and I think that she had visited Lodgemore Cloth Mill in Stroud and that she was photographed standing with the workers outside the mill. At Lister's she was transported around the extensive works in the royal auto truck, driven by Fred Evans of the auto-truck department.

In those days the company employed around 2,800 workers, the majority of whom were local, with hundreds being brought in by bus from Wotton-under-Edge, Gloucester and Stroud. All the bus timetables were arranged to suit the work people and the standard working week was forty-seven hours, Monday to Friday, starting at 7.30 a.m., dinner 12 noon to 1 p.m., afternoon 1 p.m. to 5 p.m. and Saturdays 7.30 a.m. to 12 noon.

The Red & White Bus Co. ran a regular service of three double-decker buses from Stroud to Dursley, each carrying up to sixty people, of which I was one. The buses also served the overtime shift which started at 5.15 p.m. and finished at 7.15 p.m.

My next recollection is a personal one. My father, Bill Pugh, who was fifty-seven years old in 1940, was working as a gardener and weekend park keeper at Stratford Park. I think that Mr C.E. Percy was head gardener and George Ham was head groundsman. Soon after the Second Word War started a Dig for Victory campaign was launched and it was decided that a large area of the park should be ploughed up and used for food production. My father, a farmer's son, was an expert ploughman using a horse-drawn single-furrow plough, and volunteered to do the ploughing and was loaned a plough and two draught horses by a local farmer. I recall that this created a lot of interest because more ploughing was done by tractor-drawn ploughs then.

My last recollection, again a personal one, is of the ration book used throughout the war and into the early 1950s until rationing was discontinued. It is of interest to note that supplies or rations could only be purchased from the retailer whose name appeared on the inside of the ration book.

In our case the meat ration could only be purchased from R. Hale, butcher, High Street, Stroud, and our groceries from the Star Supply Store, 4a High Street, Stroud.

My wife worked throughout the war as secretary to Mr R.E. Stuart, solicitor of Bedford Street, Stroud, and found it to be more convenient to shop in Stroud rather than Stonehouse.

5

Canals

Those Were the Days (written in 2001)

I am so pleased that the Stroudwater Canal restoration is now an established fact although sadly, at nearly eighty-six years of age, I shall not be around to witness that auspicious occasion. It is the best news heard in the Stroud Valleys for many years and will bring back prosperity, not only to Stroud itself, but also to all the delightful villages through which it passes. I have been connected with it and have enjoyed every aspect of it since I was born in the cottages adjacent to the weir at Whitminster on 8 August 1915. In 1919 my parents moved to Rose Cottage, Westend, Eastington, and then to No. 2 Council Houses, Chipman's Platt, Eastington. This was next to what was then the Workhouse, now William Morris House, and a few hundred yards from the canal.

Sadly, one of the most beautiful areas of the canal from around Westfield Bridge has been filled in to accommodate the M5 motorway. Since it was excavated in the 1790s it has been known by generations of Eastington villagers as the 'cut'. It was one of the most popular recreation spots for all age groups at a time when organised games were very few. We swam in it from the middle of June to the end of September, skated on it when it was frozen over to a depth of 5–6in for generally about three to four weeks in the very severe winters of the late 1920s and early 1930s.

In addition to this we fished in it during the season, set night lines baited with 'gudgeon' to catch eels and took moorhen eggs to eat – they were small but delicious fried in the fat left by home-cured bacon. The night lines were set on the bank opposite the towpath and a long way from the bridges. If an eel had been caught the line would be tight. This would be noticed by the dozens of men who cycled along the towpath very early in the morning to work at Cadbury's Frampton factory or canal employees based at Saul Junction.

They would jump off their bikes, cut the night line and put the eel in their dinner bags. Two or three large eels would make a meal for a family of four. The preparation of the eels for cooking was standard practice for everyone living near or passing by the canal. The eel would have swallowed the gudgeon head first and the fish hook, which together with the line, had been threaded through its body with the hook barb outside the side of the gudgeon's mouth and would first be cut from the eel's stomach together with its entrails, using a very sharp knife. A carving fork would then be stuck through the eel's head and into a wooden chopping block.

Every family had a chopping block outside their back door. It was a section of tree trunk (usually elm or beech) about 12–15in in diameter and about 18in tall. It was used to provide a platform on which to chop kindling wood; its secondary use was to hold eels. With the eel firmly impaled, again using a sharp knife, the skin behind the eel's head would be cut through. Two dinner forks would be inserted into the skin on each side of the head and a sharp simultaneous pull on both forks would remove the skin from head to tail. The skin would be cut up and given to the cat and the eels placed in a bowl of very salty water to be left to soak from twelve to twenty-four hours. They were then boiled until tender in salted water and made a cheap meal for the very poor families existing, not living, near the canal at that time. Reverting to the moorhens' eggs, the moorhens' nests were very plentiful on the bank opposite the towpath and, during the nesting season, we would visit the nests daily. We observed when the birds had commenced to lay and never took more than two eggs from each nest thus ensuring that continuity of breeding would be preserved.

It is certain that future generations of children will not be able to enjoy many of the activities I have mentioned when the canal is fully restored. However, I hope that the present generation will appreciate what a valuable recreational asset the canal was in those dim and distant years.

LIFESAVER'S CHANCE TO MAKE A SPLASH

Generations of Eastington boys learned to swim in the Stanley branch of the River Frome which flowed from Beard's Mill, near to the railway viaduct, through Millend in Eastington. This section, known as The Ketch Pools, flowed over a bed of gravel that acted as a filter leaving the water crystal clear. The depth of water in summer was about 2ft 6in deep which was ideal for boys aged eight to ten to swim in safety.

There was no formal tuition but one older boy would supervise the younger ones. No flotation aids were used and the dog paddle was the first stroke to be mastered. The older boy would put his band under the young one's chin and say 'Get your feet up and kick!' If you really wanted to swim, and most did, you could manage to dog paddle a few yards after about two weeks' tuition.

When you felt reasonably confident, you joined the older boys who were swimming in the Stroudwater Canal above Westfield Bridge; in the lock if it was full or above it if it was empty. At this stage a rope was tied under your armpits and you were supported in the very deep water by an older person and yanked out when you had taken in several mouthfuls of water. As you became more proficient and it was seen safe to do so, the rope was discarded and you were left to your own devices and to learn the various strokes as best you could. The general progression from the dog paddle was to the breast stroke, side stroke, over-arm stroke, crawl and finally the back stroke. You then learned to dive and swim under water. When you became proficient at all these strokes you felt really at home in the water.

It was then that you learned the most useful discipline of all. This was how to save a person drowning in deep water. In retrospect, this may seem to be a strange thing for a young boy of probably eleven to twelve years of age to do. However, it felt perfectly natural for us and would indicate, using today's hackneyed terminology, that all those years ago we were a 'caring society'. We were taught to approach the drowning person from behind so that he or she would not grab you and possibly drown you both. Then we either held his or her head above water with both hands while swimming to the bank using only the feet movement of the back stroke, or to hold the head above water with the left arm while swimming the side stroke with both feet and the right arm!

We practiced this extensively in the Westfield Lock, naturally with both parties being able to swim, until we had really mastered the procedure. I thought that I would never use the ability that I had gained, until one day while a pupil at Marling School in my early teens; I was swimming in the canal with the Stonehouse Swimming Club at their headquarters near the branch railway line – now the Ebley Bypass Bridge. It was then that a young lad named Gilbert Lusty from King's Stanley, who was a non-swimmer, was pushed in while fooling about on the bank.

I saw that he was on the point of drowning and, being on the towpath at the time, I dived in and swam side stroke with him to the towpath bank. After much coughing and spluttering he recovered, said thanks and went back to King's Stanley. About thirty years later in the late 1950s when I was shop superintendent in the R.A. Lister Dursley Iron Foundry, the company's personnel manager sent a big hefty man, whose name I recognised, to me for further interview for a very hot, heavy and dirty job charging materials into the Cupola Melting Furnaces. I considered that he was suitable for the job and advised him that he could start immediately. He then said, 'Are you Mr Les Pugh from Eastington?' I said 'Yes'. He said, 'do you remember when you saved my life in the cut?' This brought memories flooding back and we had a brief chat about the incident.

The whole point of this little story is to implore all those very able young swimmers of today to learn life-saving. You never know when it may prove to be useful.

Secrets of the Lost Waterway

In the 1960s I was friendly with Bob Boakes who lived with his family at Valley View, Bridgend. Bob, like myself, was very interested in the Kemmett canal which formed the boundary at the bottom of his garden. He had made an in-depth research into the history of the waterway, about which very little is known.

The objective of Mr Kemmett's canal was to utilise the River Frome to transport coal from the Forest of Dean and the Midlands to the many woollen-cloth mills built on the River Frome. Originally they used water wheels to provide the power for the weaving looms, but had changed to steam power as a more reliable source of energy.

Because of opposition from mill owners at the use of locks to accommodate the rising levels of the valley, Mr Kemmett devised a scheme which would eliminate locks by creating 'pounds' on the new waterway. Double-headed cranes were used to lift 1-ton wooden containers carried in barges from the lower level to barges at the higher level.

The Kemmett started at Ryeford and the first identifiable lifting station is at Downton Road, Bridgend, where the river changes its level and direction. The next lifting station is at Lower Mills, Bridgend, where there is a weir and the remains of the lifting station. From there the next lifting station is at Beard's Mill which is adjacent to the railway viaduct and has a weir. This station would have served Bond's Mill. After Bond's Mill, the best-preserved weir and lifting station is at Churchend, Eastington. This would have served the now derelict Churchend Mill. From Churchend, the next identifiable weir and lifting station is at Fromebridge Mill.

From Whitminster, Kemmett used the Cambridge Canal, which was in use from about 1740 and provided a navigable waterway to the River Severn at Framilode. Mr Kemmett started his canal in 1758 but it had a short life and was abandoned in 1763. The Stroudwater Canal was started in 1775 and abandoned in 1933.

ELVERS WERE PLENTIFUL AND WERE SOLD FOR 2D A PINT

As I have mentioned in previous articles, my profoundly deaf father was sent in the First World War to manage the farm and estate of the Teesdale family of Whitminster House. This house had been the residence of the Lord of the Manor for several centuries. In the mid-1700s, the then Lord of the Manor at Whitminster House was Richard Owen Cambridge. He, with several others, financed an operation to make the River Frome navigable from Framilode to the Bristol Road.

I can distinctly remember that the river was tidal up to the weir. The weir split the excess water when the balancing ponds above it were full. These ponds were used to top up the water level in the section of the canal from the recently excavated Whitminster lock to Saul Junction. The Perrett family, who lived in the house above the weir, were in charge of this operation. The ponds were filled by the River Frome which passed through an aqueduct under the Stroudwater Canal about 500yds above the Whitminster Lock.

At the period I am describing, elvers in the River Severn were very plentiful and a considerable quantity travelled up the Frome as far as the weir when the tides were high. Sometimes, my father would catch a considerable quantity. Elvers were always sold by the pint. The price at that time was 2d for one pint.

On the subject of the use of wind power, there were two wind-driven water pumps situated between Whitminster House and the Bristol Road. Both were used to pump the water from the well above which they were located; one to Whitminster House, and the other to Parklands which was then occupied by the Ormrod family. They were probably erected during the reign of Queen Victoria and were made by John

Wallace Titt of Warminster in Wiltshire. The wind-driven rotor was about 7-8ft in diameter and had multiple tapered blades which were attached to a substantial circular ring of the diameter mentioned. At the centre, the blades were attached to an equally substantial hub. The shaft to which the hub was attached was cranked between its two retaining bearings. The depth of crank was about 6in, which meant that the vertical pump shaft attached to the crank had a stroke of 12in when the cranked shaft rotated.

The whole of this assembly was supported by a steel structure similar to a small electricity pylon. It was about 20ft high and had a steel ladder attached which permitted access to the rotor which could be locked.

To end, I would ask those readers who are interested to be tolerant, it was a long time ago and while I believe the above to be true, I have no means of checking it.

Bus Service Took Trade from Traditional Canal Steam Boats

For this latest snippet of nostalgia I want to take you back to 1919 when I was four years old and lived at Whitminster. To continue my memories of travel at that period, the following paints a true picture of the way we lived.

The outlying villages in the Severn Vale had one very popular way of getting to Gloucester. This was on the Berkeley, Gloucester to Sharpness Canal. There were two Wave and Lapwing steam-driven boats. They were well-patronised by the people who lived near the canal and they were stopping places all the way up the canals, generally near to bridges.

My family – father, mother, elder brother and myself – lived in a tied cottage belonging to the Lord of the Manor, the Revd Teesdale of Whitminster House. My profoundly deaf father, the son of a sheep farmer, was deemed unfit for military service in the First World War and was directed to Whitminster House to manage the farm with the assistance of two Land Army girls. He was also verger, bell ringer, sexton and grave digger at Whitminster Church in which I was christened.

Returning to the Wave and Lapwing, my mother would take me to the bridge over the Stroudwater Canal and along the towpath to Saul Junction where we would cross the Berkeley Canal on the footbridge and wait at the landing stage on the Gloucester side. There would generally be five or six people from Frampton, Saul, Arlingham, Epney, Longney and Whitminster waiting here. The journey to Gloucester would take two hours or more, depending on the number of stops the boats had to make. On Saturdays the boats, which had two decks, would be full of passengers.

It was about at that time that the Blue Taxis bus service started running between Gloucester and Bristol on what was then known as the Bristol Road, now the A38. Later the Silvey family started to run a bus service from Epney to Gloucester and the Lewis family ran a bus from Frampton to Stroud (I think).

This new-fangled, but less comfortable form of transport was very much quicker and more convenient than the canal steam boats which soon lost all their trade and the service was discontinued. After Gloucester, the place most frequently visited was

Stonehouse. It had two railway stations and shops that sold most things needed by simple country folk. A carrier service to Stonehouse from Frampton-on-Severn via School Lane, Whitminster and Grove Lane through Westend, Eastington, was operated by Mr Betteridge with his pony and trap. He would take people and goods to any destination en route. One of his main functions was to collect domestic servants and their boxes containing all their worldly goods from the railway stations to take up employment in the many great houses of the aristocracy in the area. Mr Betteridge's fees for carrying these girls going into domestic service were paid by their employer's housekeeper when he delivered them to their destination. When my mother wished to visit Stonehouse she would arrange for Mr Betteridge to pick us up. We would sit on the wooden seat across the trap next to him, which again was most uncomfortable.

In late 1919 my family moved from Whitminster to Westend, Eastington, so that my father could work for a gentleman farmer, Melville Wight of Westend Farm. They had been friends for some time and played skittles together. Melville sublet two orchards to my father to enable him to keep poultry and pigs and also to make cider and perry. He was able to make many gallons of each drink. The apples for the cider and the pears for the perry were taken by horse and cart to Mr White of Fromebridge Mill who provided a cider-making service for all the local farmers and smallholders. My father usually had about 60 gallons of cider and 40 gallons of perry made each year. Both were contained in wooden casks made by Coopers' very skilled men. Each cask had a large bunghole in the side and a much smaller tap hole in the end.

The casks were trammed in our back kitchen in which the coal was stacked in a wooden enclosure. The cider and perry was drunk from a tot made of cow's horn. The tot was always left upside down on one of the wooden taps in the casks. Nearly all the tradesmen who called with supplies helped themselves to cider or perry at my father's invitation. This may seem to be inconceivably unhygienic but the tot was never washed. Before each individual drank from it a small quantity of cider or perry would be swilled around the tot and thrown onto the coal. They would then sit on a wooden bench and enjoy the drink.

The people I can remember enjoying this facility were Joe Dowding, the Co-op horse and cart bread-delivery man, Mr Davis, the postman from Stonehouse, and Mr Hobbs, who delivered paraffin carried in what I think were converted milk churns with taps fitted. Mr Davis rode a red bicycle and Mr Hobbs used a horse and cart.

TRIALS AND TRIBULATIONS ON THE STROUDWATER CANAL

For this next series of reminiscences of the Stroudwater Canal in the 1920s we will move from Eastington C of E School at Churchend to the Pike Bridge and the now non-existent Coal Wharf to the west of it. It would be true to say that, next to Westfield Bridge, this is the area with which I was most familiar. The Pike Bridge was so-named because a turnpike and house stood there before the arrival of the 'cut'.

The Wharf was opened on 1 January 1778 as a depot for general cargo brought up the canal on Severn trows and was used to store timber, stone and bricks for use in the construction of the canal from Pike Lock to Blunder Lock and onwards. As the canal construction progressed, it was used solely as a coal wharf. From about the late 1880s, it was rented from the Canal company by Zachaeus Whiting.

I am not certain which name was correct, but in 1920 everyone knew him as Zaccy Whiting. He had a long white beard, was exceptionally religious – even for that period – and frequently preached the gospel at Nupend Baptist Church. Zaccy owned a narrow boat which he named *Nellie* – crewed by Mr and Mrs Stephen Chandler who made it their home and spent all their working life on it. They travelled between Eastington Wharf and Coppice Colliery, which I think is near Cannock in Staffordshire – a journey which could take weeks. They started from Eastington with *Nellie* being towed by a mule to the junction with the Berkeley Canal at Saul. Here, the mule would be put out to graze and *Nellie*, with two or three other narrow boats, would be towed by steam tug to Gloucester Docks, then up the River Severn and Midland canals to Coppice Colliery. Then she was loaded by hand by two men carrying the coal in a hog or hand barrow on a plank of wood on the edge of the wharf and the side of the barge. When the barge was fully loaded, the entire cargo would be 'sheeted' with made-to-measure canvas sheets. I was told that the sheeting not only protected the coal, but also prevented it from being stolen during the night on the journey. Nothing travelled on inland waterways during the hours of darkness.

This would be an opportune time to explain why Zaccy chose to purchase his coal from Staffordshire when there were adequate supplies much nearer in the Forest of Dean. I am not qualified to guarantee the accuracy of this statement, but all those years ago, I was told that Forest coal was 'hard' coal which needed considerable draught – passage of air through it – to ensure combustion was maintained, whereas the 'soft' Staffordshire coal would burn with practically no draught. The hard coal was then known as 'steam' coal because it was ideal for use in steam-raising factories and mill boilers, where a strong draught was induced by the very tall factory or mill chimneys, as featured in Lowry paintings. The soft Staffordshire coal was known as house coal.

On arrival at Eastington Wharf the coal was unloaded using a hog carried by two men and stacked. Zaccy used casual labour for this purpose. One worker was named George Baltic Smith (he was an ex-naval man who had served on the Baltic). The other was Cocker Woodman (he was cross-eyed). They were very tough and I was frightened of them both.

When Zaccy had paid them for their work, they would walk along the towpath to the New Inn at Newtown. Mrs Duxbury was the landlady and could handle any situation. Barrie and Cocker would get blind drunk which, sadly, was the only pleasure in their very hard life.

The following incident which I am about to relate is, to the best of my knowledge, not recorded in any of the many excellent books written about the canal and probably I am the only living person to have knowledge of it.

As I have mentioned *Nellie* was crewed by Mr and Mrs Chandler. Both, like Zaccy, were very religious and almost as old as he was. At that time, narrow boats owned by James Smart of Chalford far outnumbered the other boats on the canal and were crewed by much younger and aggressive men. They dominated the canal at the time and would prevent *Nellie* gaining access to the lock chambers on the return trip when empty. This would mean that *Nellie* was too late to pick up the steam tug at Saul Junction and would have to wait for weeks before the next tug became available. This incensed Zaccy but, because of his principles, he would not take any direct action. However, to show his displeasure, he had *Nellie* renamed *Live and Let Live* and I can distinctly remember the sign writer making the alteration while the barge was waiting at the wharf.

The sign writer was a barge artist. I would think the date would be 1922 or 1923. After the death of Zaccy a few years later, Mr and Mrs Chandler retired – where to I don't know, but I sincerely hope that it was not to the adjacent workhouse! *Live and Let Live* was sold and no doubt the first thing the new owner did was to have it renamed!

MEMORIES OF CANAL LIFE (WRITTEN IN 2006)

The wonderful news that the Stroudwater Canal restoration project has at last been promised an immense amount of capital has induced me to write a few more memories – some with the aid of Key's *A History of Eastington* first printed in 1953.

In the 1920s and early 1930s I lived with my parents at Chipman's Platt. The dry dock and maintenance yard were located there and, although now in my ninety-first year, I have vivid memories of the activities I witnessed there.

Among the streams diverted by the cutting of the canal was Oldbury Brook. The channel alongside the road where it joined the canal – weir water – is still called 'the divers' (the divert). At the junction of the divers with the canal a boathouse sheltered the 'ice breaker' until both decayed with age and exposure.

Last used in January or February 1895 the ice breaker was a stoutly built boat of the width of our largest coal barge. It was towed by a rope on the bow and rocked by a rope on a short masthead (both by manpower from the towpath) so that the beam ends projecting tooth-like at water level moved up and down tilting and breaking the ice sheets.

The dry dock which was used for worship by Baptists in 1871 when Nupend Chapel was being rebuilt, stood between the canal from which it was filled and 'the divers' into which it was emptied, both by gravity. A high roof covered with wooden shingles gave ample clearance for vessel shipwrights and repairing gear.

A clock turret rose above the up-stream gable and the large clock face gave the time unofficially to passengers over the Pike Bridge and officially to the lock keeper in his house, telling him when to affix and when to remove from the nearest lock gate the padlock that immobilised shipping during the hours of darkness and over Sundays.

6

TRANSPORT

TRAVEL WAS A MATTER OF CLASS

The RAC Foundation, in its report *Maturing Towards 2050* predicts that, as travel has trebled in the past fifty years with 85 per cent of it by car, by 2031 car travel could be nearly 50 per cent higher.

These frightening statistics have prompted me to cast my mind back eighty years or more. In those far-off days, travel as we know it did not exist. It is true to say that 75 per cent of people living in what were then the isolated villages of Whitminster and Eastington never travelled further than Gloucester. Only the rich travelled, the poor stayed at home. Travel to the poor was the distance they were able to walk, or in a very few cases, cycle. While most village people worked on the land or in 'service' in the large houses of the aristocracy, the adventurous few were prepared to walk long distances to work in mills and factories where they could earn more money.

Using my own experience at my late employer R.A. Lister & Co. Ltd as an example, many of the elderly men working there when I joined the company in September 1931 had for many years walked regularly from Wotton-under-Edge and Nympsfield to Dursley. This was before the advent of local buses and only the use of public footpaths made both journeys possible. In each case the distance walked by footpath was probably not much more than half the distance if the roads had been used.

To own a bicycle in those days meant saving up for many months, possibly years. Hire purchase had not then been an option. A new bicycle cost £3 19s 6d for a single-gear machine, while an extra £1 bought a three-speed machine. While the following observances are not directly related to travel, they paint a true picture of life at that time.

In the late 1920s and early 1930s, a skilled foundry man who had served a seven-year indentured apprenticeship was paid £2 16s for a forty-seven-hour week, while an unskilled labourer was paid £1 18s for the same hours.

Players Navy Cut and Wills Gold Flake cigarettes cost 1s for a packet of twenty. Woodbines were the working man's smoke (five for 2d in a green paper packet). Smoking cigarettes or a pipe was considered to be beneficial to one's health, in fact it had a calming effect. In fact, smoking and drinking cider at 4d a pint were the only pleasures enjoyed by the relatively poor at that time.

A Learning Curve for Motorists

Motoring is the subject for this bit of nostalgia. I am one of the few remaining car drivers who has not taken or passed a driving test and although I have driven safely during the last sixty-three years, I am certain that I would fail if I had to take a test now.

In 1940 when I started driving there were few driving schools operating and financial constraints meant that most learner drivers were self-taught and had only the experience of the accompanying qualified drivers. We naturally studied the Highway Code then in use. In the early 1940s, when instructors and examiners had been called up to serve, the law was changed to permit all drivers then holding a provisional driving licence to drive unaccompanied by a qualified driver. The law was again amended after the war to allow all learners throughout the war years to obtain a full driving licence when they next applied.

In 1940 I purchased a blue 1934 Standard Nine saloon registration number DG9007. I bought it from Cyril Cripps, a fellow R.A. Lister employee who lived at Middleyard between King's Stanley and Selsley. I paid him £19 for it and sold it for £40 in 1942. I bought a Morris 8 saloon in 1942, registration number AUE374 for which I paid £50.

I am going to record my memories of the Standard Nine which was made at Coventry sixty-nine years ago by the now defunct Standard Motor Co. Like most of the cheaper small cars it had a side-valve engine. The 'Nine' indicates that the cubic capacity of the engine was about 900cc. Such was the inefficiency of the side-valve engine that the power output was about 27 brake hp. It was a two-door saloon, had a fabric sliding roof which leaked in very heavy rain, there was no boot and the spare wheel was carried on a bracket at the back of the car. It had wire-spoked wheels with cross-ply tyres and inner tubes. It had cable brakes to all four wheels which were satisfactory in summer but in winter the water which entered the cable sheath froze solid. This meant that the car could not be driven until the ice had been melted by heating the sheaths with a paraffin blowlamp.

Lubricating oil technology was not very advanced. An oil of normal viscosity was used in summer while a much thinner oil such as Castrolite was used during the winter. Progressive cylinder wear increased the consumption of lubricating oil to an unacceptable degree so I had the engine rebored and oversize pistons and rings fitted. The rebore was done at Les Hill's Stonehouse garage which was where the Bethel Church and Billiard Club now stand. It was done by Norman White, an engineer at Steels Garage of Russell Street, Stroud. The garage was where the Stroud and Swindon Building Society office stands now.

Norman, then in his mid-sixties, would take a portable boring machine to any garage and, using a single-point tool, would enlarge each bore until the ovality which he had previously checked with an internal micrometer had been removed. Les Hill and Bert Willcox then rebuilt the engine fitting new pistons and rings which suited the new diameter. After reboring, the engine had to be run in very carefully with a lubricating oil which carried graphite in suspension. When a specified mileage had been recorded this oil was drained off and a flushing oil was used before filling the sump with the appropriate grade of lubricating oil for the time of year.

CAR-SPOTTING DAYS

During the 1920s when I was a pupil at Eastington C of E School and, with a few other boys of my age group, I used to record in a notebook the registration number and make of any motor which I had seen. In those far-off days the number of horse-drawn vehicles far exceeded the number of motor cars seen in rural villages like Eastington. The 'car-spotting' activity was at its height in what was known as the August holiday which was of four weeks' duration.

After the holidays those of us who enjoyed this hobby would compare our notes. I have to admit that generally I had recorded far more registration numbers and makes of car than most of my fellow pupils. The reason for this was that I was living at Chipman's Platt, next to the workhouse which is now William Morris House, and it was a short walk along the Stroudwater Canal towpath to the Bristol Road at Whitminster, now classified as the A38. I found out that I could see and record more motor cars on this road in one day than I could in a whole week at Eastington.

Mr H.S. Hack, who as the owner of Bourne Mill in Brimscombe, which produced walking and umbrella sticks, lived at The Grove, Westend, Eastington, originally had a Crossley four-seat soft-topped luxury car and later on one of the very first Bean 14 saloons produced at Tipton in what is now the West Midlands.

The other cars seen in the village were Hamptons manufactured at Dudbridge, near Stroud, Model T Fords which were imported from the USA and a few three-wheeled, air-cooled Morgans which were made at Malvern in Worcestershire (I think!). There were also one or two chain-driven Trojans.

Of all the cars seen in the village, by far the most impressive was a deep purple Daimler limousine owned by Sir Percival Marling VC of Stanley Park, Selsley, near Stroud. This was driven by his chauffeur dressed in an elegant uniform of the same colour with a peaked cap to match.

To end these pleasant memories of times long past I must mention the Brough Superior hand-built British superbike and Indian and Harley Davidson from the USA which were in the same category.

A Hampton Car being tested on the Nailsworth Ladder. (Courtesy Dr Ray Wilson of the Gloucestershire Society for Industrial Archaeology)

Motorbikes were Popular

For this next instalment of my reminiscences, I want to start where I left off, in the 1920s.

Eastington at this time had more than its share of families living below the poverty line. I could write an account of deprivation which would be hardly believable today. The early years of that decade were very austere. The First World War had ended on 11 November 1918. Standish Hospital was full of ex-soldiers whose health had been ruined by the horrors of life in the trenches. Sadly, the majority did not survive.

Working people's greatest fear was being ill and needing a doctor. There was no national health insurance and the thought of having to pay a doctor's bill was frightening for the poor. Consequently the mortality rate among the poor was greatly in excess of those who were better off.

At the other end of the social scale, the more adventurous of the gentry and a few reasonably well-off individuals were beginning to move from the traditional horse-drawn transport to petrol-driven vehicles. There were probably no more than five car owners in the village.

Of these, the Rector of Eastington, the Revd George Thomas Altimus Ward, was the most enthusiastic. His first car was a French-built MORS with the registration number AD1. This was the very first registration of any motor vehicle in the county of Gloucestershire.

Cars registered in the city of Gloucester carried the registration letters FH. The second car owned by Revd Ward was one of the first Baby Austin cars built at Longbridge in Birmingham. It was a soft-topped model and its registration number was DF1. In county of Gloucestershire the letters AD were used until the numbers reached 9999. After this the prefix letters were changed to DD, DF, DG.

George de Lisle Bush of The Leaze owned a Sunbeam luxury saloon car which was driven by his chauffeur Jimmy Twiselton.

Turning to motor cycles, these were quite expensive but greatly sought after by young men in their early twenties. To own one meant saving up for a considerable time purchasing a second-hand machine.

The most popular makes were Cotton which were made in Gloucester, Douglas which were made at Kingswood in Bristol, followed by BSA, Norton, Triumph, AJS, Aerial, Rudge, Whitworth, Dunelt, New Imperial and New Hudson. The Co-op also sold a small two-stroke machine which they named Federation.

In addition there were a few high-performance machines made locally by H.P. Baughn of Lansdown, Stroud. These were slightly more expensive but much sought after by enthusiasts like Ron Johnson and Tom Powles who were star players in Stroud's Motor Cycle football team. This sport, which was played at Fromehall Park, was extremely popular in the 1920s and the Stroud team was considered to be the best in the country.

Pugh family Hillman Californian car with daughter Rosemary and miniature poodle Twinkle.

It's Worth Waiting for Morris

The outline described here was really the first of this nature I had been able to enjoy since the outbreak of the Second World War. Nine years, even in those days, seemed to be a long, long time. Everything was rationed, especially petrol, and new cars had been unavailable since 1940.

After the war ended in 1945 the basic petrol ration was increased sufficiently to make pleasure motoring possible again, and, when it was announced that a motor show was to be held at Earl's Court, we could hardly wait to see the new models that were to be exhibited. I was a dedicated Morris owner and was running a very reliable black, four-door Series E Morris 8 made in 1940. Its registration number was EDD98 and I had purchased it for £200 from Eddie Lundegaard when his business was based in Barton Street.

The car I had set my heart on was the new Morris Minor. Its shape was attractive to the eye and there seemed to be no doubt that the traditional Morris reliability would be maintained. My friend and immediate superior in the R.A. Lister's Iron Foundry at Dursley, Parnal Vigar, who had been fortunate enough to have purchased a brand new Series E Morris 8 manufactured in 1947, was also keen to visit the motor show. He thought that it would be a pleasant outing for my wife Peggy and suggested that she should invite a friend to accompany her on a shopping trip in the West End while we enjoyed ourselves at the Motor Show.

Peggy invited her best friend Mary Davis, who lived at Bussage and worked with Peggy as a legal secretary employed by Mr R.E. Stuart, a respected solicitor who had his office in Bedford Street, Stroud. Parnal and I agreed that we would commit our basic ration petrol coupons for the trip to London using his new car which had never undertaken a long journey. We set off quite early on the first Saturday morning of the show, drove down the Thames Valley route as far as Kew, where we parked the Morris in a garage and proceeded to Earl's Court on the underground.

It was about midday when we arrived and were surprised at the length of the queues waiting for admission. When we did get inside, the main hall was so crowded we were unable to get anywhere near to the most popular exhibits, of which the Morris Minor was one. The only way we could see it was from the galleries which exhibited accessories – we did eventually get a look at it in the late afternoon when the crowds had thinned.

We had a pleasant journey home, including a meal at the Trout Inn, Lechlade. The following Monday I telephoned the Wicliffe Garage, then located in Russell Street where Peacock's Store now stands, and placed a firm order for a new Morris Minor. Believe it or not, the car was ordered in October 1948 and was not delivered until 23 June 1952 and I paid £593. Its registration number was LDG499 and it was a two-door saloon with red upholstery. By today's standard it was very spartan; there was no heater, radio or demister and the seats were rather hard. Nevertheless it was the realisation of a long-term ambition starting in the dark days of 1940. I was truly thankful and lavished every care on it until I traded it in for £300 in 1955 when I purchased an as-new blue and cream Hillman Californian for £550 from Steels Garage then located at the top of Russell Street.

Les with his Gloucestershire Medal of Courage Award, April 2005.

7

LES – A MAN OF COURAGE

BRAVE LES UP FOR COURAGE MEDAL

Below is an article that was published in the *Stroud News & Journal* on 6 April 2005:

BRAVE Stonehouse pensioner Les Pugh has been nominated for a prestigious award after being targeted by criminals three times in one year.

The well-known town resident, 89, was nominated for the Gloucestershire Medal of Courage by Stonehouse Town Council after enduring what he called 'the worst year of my life'.

But on Monday he modestly said he was 'amazed' that his name had been put forward for the gong, awarded every year by Gloucestershire County Council.

On the first occasion his home was burgled, then crooks stole hundreds of pounds from his bank account.

But on a third occasion he stood up to another suspected confidence trickster and managed to turn him away

To add to his dreadful year, Mr Pugh also suffered the loss of his beloved wife Peggy after 65 years of marriage.

In recognition of his courage, Stroud MP and Stonehouse Town Councillor David Drew, suggested his nomination, which was warmly endorsed by his fellow councillors.

'It was a big surprise – I am amazed,' said Mr Pugh. 'I do not think I did anything above what anybody else would normally do. I think 2004 was the worst year of my life. It was a bad year – but I am still here.'

The courageous pensioner will now have to wait until September 21 to find out if he has won a medal. Usually only two are awarded each year.

Any organisation or individual can nominate a Gloucestershire resident for the medals if they think they deserve recognition.

One medal is normally for either an act of gallantry or self-sacrifice, the other for moral courage and bravery.

LES MAKES A SPLASH

The article below was published in the *Stroud News & Journal* on 10 August 2005:

Determined pensioner Les Pugh made a splash when he took part in a sponsored swim in aid of the World Cancer Research Fund.

Regular *SNJ* writer Les, 90, completed a remarkable sponsored swim at Stratford Park Leisure Centre on Monday.

Les, a former bowel cancer sufferer himself, overcame the illness in 2001 and has since made an annual donation to the charity.

Despite arthritis in his shoulders, Les completed four lengths of the pool using mainly backstroke, accompanied by his granddaughter, Limara Davis, 20, and her friend, 17-year-old Stacey Phillips.

Limara's fiancé Benn May watched the swim accompanied by Pete Wilson of BBC Radio Gloucestershire, the organiser of the event.

When asked why he wanted to do the swim, Les simply replied he wanted to help other cancer sufferers get through the disease.

The cash from his swim is still being counted. Any future donations to the charity can be sent to the World Cancer Research Fund, Freepost, SR9 9AD

Les and his granddaughter, Limara Davis, at Stratford Park Leisure Centre, August 2005.

Other local titles published by The History Press

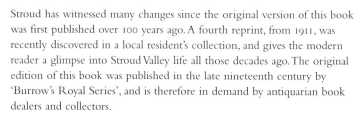

Mr Pedersen A Man of Genius
DAVID EVANS

Born in Denmark in 1855, Mikael Pedersen is known for his bicycle of unusual design – the Dursley Pedersen. At the end of that war he vanished and the rest of his life was for a long time a mystery. What happened to him was first revealed in this author's The Ingenious Mr Pedersen, published in 1978. In this present book David Evans tells Mikael's unusual story again with much more information.

978 0 7524 4505 2

The Stroud Valley Illustrated

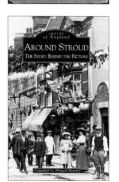

Stroud has witnessed many changes since the original version of this book was first published over 100 years ago. A fourth reprint, from 1911, was recently discovered in a local resident's collection, and gives the modern reader a glimpse into Stroud Valley life all those decades ago. The original edition of this book was published in the late nineteenth century by 'Burrow's Royal Series', and is therefore in demand by antiquarian book dealers and collectors.

978 0 7524 4817 6

Around Stroud The Story Behind The Picture
HOWARD BEARD

Around Stroud recalls some of the events and personalities which shaped the Stroud area in the early twentieth century. Amongst the 100 old pictures and other archive ephemera which illustrate this volume are snapshots of the arrival of the first railcars and motor buses as well as photographs of Coronation celebrations, May Day revels and Empire Day festivities, the Great Snow of 1916 and Red Cross Hospitals.

978 0 7524 1577 2

Stroud Streets and Shops
WILF MERRETT

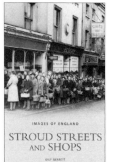

With over 150 photographs, postcards and advertisements, Stroud Streets and Shops captures the town's commercial heritage. At the beginning of the twentieth century, there were a number of shops in Stroud offering everything the casual shopper or housewife needed. The town has seen many changes since then and this book recalls Stroud in the days before the arrival of supermarkets and shopping malls.

978 0 7524 3307 3

If you are interested in purchasing other books published by The History Press, or in case you have difficulty finding any History Press books in your local bookshop, you can also place orders directly through our website
www.thehistorypress.co.uk